Cooking With the Chiles & Spices of

MEXICO

Cooking With the Chiles & Spices of

MEXICO

56 Recipes Exploring the Culinary Secrets of Mexico

INTRODUCTION BY KATHLEEN O'ROURKE

♦

RECIPES BY

KATHLEEN O'ROURKE & JULIA SCANNELL

Published by
Culinary Alchemy®, Inc.
Post Office Box 393
Palo Alto, California
94302
1.800.424.0005
Manufactured in the United States.

Editor: Elizabeth Connolly
Design: Elizabeth Ives Manwaring
San Rafael, California

ISBN 0-9647724-1-8

First Edition

THIS BOOK WAS WRITTEN FOR THOSE WHO KNOW
A CULTURE'S FOOD IS THE FIRST KEY TO UNDERSTANDING ITS PEOPLE.

MANY THANKS TO OUR TALENTED GUIDES: RICARDO MUÑOZ, CARMEN
RAMÍREZ AND ESPECIALLY MÓNICA MASTRETTA TIBURCIO,
WHOSE ENTHUSIASM FOR SHARING PUEBLA'S SECRETS MADE THE TOWN'S
EXPLORATION A SPECIAL EXPERIENCE FOR US ALL.
THANKS ALSO GO TO MARILYN TAUSEND, WHO ORGANIZED OUR RAPID BUT
THOROUGH JOURNEY THROUGH CENTRAL MEXICO.

OUR LOVE AND APPRECIATION MUST ALSO BE NOTED
FOR FAMILY AND FRIENDS WHO TESTED AND TASTED THROUGHOUT
THE BOOK'S CREATION:
JACK SHERIDAN, KEVIN PRUESSNER, KAREN MALIK,
MARY O'ROURKE & MATT HALL

About Culinary Alchemy

IN 1993, CULINARY ALCHEMY WAS FOUNDED ON THE PRINCIPLE THAT BUSY PEOPLE HAVE BEEN DOOMED TO UNINTERESTING AND EVEN UNHEALTHY FOOD FOR TOO LONG. THE LACK OF TIME IN MOST OF OUR LIVES MAKES IT DIFFICULT TO PURSUE NEW INTERESTS IN FOODS, ESPECIALLY THOSE FROM FARAWAY PLACES WITH UNFAMILIAR INGREDIENTS. OUR PRODUCTS ARE COLLECTIONS OF THE FRESHEST INGREDIENTS FOR AUTHENTIC ETHNIC COOKING, IDENTIFIED AND ACCOMPANIED BY CULTURAL RECIPES FOR THEIR USE. PEOPLE WHO HAVE LIVED IN AREAS UNCOMPROMISED BY FASTER WAYS OF EATING RETAIN THE SECRETS OF THEIR ANCESTORS IN FOOD PREPARATION AND FLAVOR COMBINATIONS. WE ALWAYS EMPHASIZE RECIPES THAT EMBODY THE INTELLIGENCE OF A COUNTRY'S HOME CHEFS. THE RESULTS FOR YOU ARE EXQUISITE MEALS WITH FLAVORS THAT RING TRUE.

Kathleen O.

KATHLEEN O'ROURKE SHERIDAN

FOUNDER

CULINARY ALCHEMY®, INC.

FOR INFORMATION ABOUT CULINARY ALCHEMY'S PRODUCTS, CALL 1.800.424.0005

Contents

Creating the Mexican Flavor — Ingredients & Preparation Techniques

KATHLEEN O'ROURKE

Corn, chiles, squash, beans, tomatoes, pumpkin seeds, potatoes, chocolate and turkey are all New World foods. To this Aztecan pantry, the Spanish conquest during the 1500s initiated a steady stream of European influence. Baked goods, cilantro, cumin, citrus fruits, almonds, rice, pork and the meat of other domesticated animals intermingled with New World foods, forming the underpinnings of today's Mexican cuisine. Lard rendered from the pig made frying a "new" cooking method available to a previously fat-free repertoire of culinary techniques. While some of these foreign influences were readily adopted, Mexico's population has remained amazingly loyal to pre-Columbian food preparation methods that are as old as the cornfields on the high plateaus surrounding Mexico City.

With the reverence of their forebears, Mexican cooks carefully cultivate and blend the flavors of their ingredients. Tomatoes, onions and garlic are roasted to mellow the vegetables into sweet, rich flavors. Toasted and ground nuts add deep flavor tones and thicken sauces. Spices, nuts, corn and even tomatoes are ground on a "metate y mano." This Aztecan food processor, a four-legged volcanic stone, allows flavors to be blended in a way not easily duplicated by modern kitchen equipment. Crushing and smashing against the stone draws out each food's essence, unlike the chopping action of a blender's metal blades.

The full complement of Mexican preparation techniques—dry sautéing pastes, roasting vegetables, toasting spices and frying purées and chiles—work together to remove bitterness from raw ingredients. The rounded, full flavors of the resulting dishes register in the mouth completely and satisfyingly. To learn these techniques in a relatively short period of time, try the recipe for Roasted Turkey with Mole Poblano on page 77. As you prepare each ingredient, take the time to relish in its aroma and changing color. When the recipe is completed, you will have gained intimate knowledge on how to draw the best flavor from each ingredient, as well as how to strike the perfect balance among them.

"Mise en place" is the cooking term that describes the advance preparation of the recipe's ingredients. Before cooking, read the recipe entirely. Prepare each ingredient as it is called for on the list—fry the chiles, chop the onion, toast and grind the spices, make the bitter orange juice, etc. The items that are processed together may be grouped in one dish or bowl. This is a helpful technique for any cuisine, saving you from mistakes and unnecessary stress.

♦ Another helpful hint is to photocopy the pages of all the recipes required for your menu. This will make it much easier to reference instructions for several recipes that are in process simultaneously.

The Characteristics of Mexican Ingredients

Many Mexican ingredients are harvested from plants originally bred in pre-Aztecan times. Indians in the valley of Mexico developed plants that not only flourished in diverse microclimates, but satisfied a range of culinary preferences. Like magic, these men and women produced corn in a rainbow of colors, fleshy squashes with various flavors and uses, 50 types of beans and as many as 200 varieties of chiles. Symbiotic relationships among plants were also utilized. Depleted cornfields were reinvigorated by the nitrogen-releasing root systems of beans. Chiles, tomatillos and squash were also grown amongst the corn, creating a self-supporting ecosystem of nutrients and shade. Today, "criollo" refers to plants cultivated in this holistic fashion, with no artificial fertilizers or pesticides. The plants yield small, imperfect, but highly flavorful crops, with little more than attentive hoeing and garden planning by the farmer. Criollo vegetables are prized by Mexican cooks, and dishes created from the field's bounty are common in home cooking, referred to as "de milpa," or "of the cornfield." In the Mexican kitchen, flavorful produce and a delightful array of seasonings combine to create robust, complex flavors in a variety of dishes prepared throughout the country.

ALLSPICE ("PIMIENTA GORDA")

Called "fat pepper" in Mexico, the English name refers to allspice's flavor, a combination of nutmeg, cinnamon and cloves. Allspice berries vary radically in size. When counting berries for a recipe, note the average size and compensate accordingly. A volatile spice, use allspice freshly ground when required.

ANISEED ("ANÍS")

Aniseed's licorice flavor imparts a bit of sweetness to savory dishes. Beans in Broth (page 114), roasted meat and some moles especially benefit from its flavor. After grinding, aniseed's intensity dissipates quickly, so use freshly ground.

ANNATTO ("ACHIOTE")

Cultivated by the Aztecs for its beautiful blossoms, the annatto tree also yields prickly pods enclosing deeply colored red seeds. Ground into the distinctive marinades of the Yucatán, the seeds infuse their subtly astringent flavor and rich color into classic dishes. See the recipe for Yucatecan Achiote Paste on page 21.

BANANA LEAVES ("HOJAS DE PLÁTANOS")

Used in central and southern Mexico, banana leaves impart a unique, smoky green flavor and aroma to the foods they enclose. The leaves are available frozen in Mexican and Asian markets, usually in 1-pound quantities. To use, the leaves must be thawed and then seared to soften. (See page 17 for preparation instructions.) After locating a source for the leaves and preparing them once, subsequent use will seem simple, and the added flavor a necessity.

BAY LEAVES, MARJORAM & THYME ("OLORES")

Use the aromatic leaf of the California bay laurel tree whole or torn into large pieces. California bay leaves, the type used in Mexico and in this book, are twice as strong as the more commonly found Turkish variety. Marjoram and thyme often join bay leaves in the group of "olores," or aromatics, commonly used in Mexican pickles, broths and marinades.

"CAL" (SLAKED LIME)

Calcium hydroxide, or "cal," can be found at hardware stores and Mexican markets. Mexicans use it to treat dried corn, as it aids in the removal of the skin, a necessary step before processing the corn into "nixtamal" (see page 14).

"CANELA" (TRUE CINNAMON)

The hard cinnamon sticks sold in supermarkets are actually cassia, true cinnamon's Chinese cousin. True cinnamon originated in Sri Lanka. Its easily-broken quills and subtle, sweet, lemony flavor are considered a necessity for Mexican dishes of all sorts, from savory to sweet. Cassia is not a substitute for canela.

In Mexico, cheese is not melted with indiscretion over every dish. Instead, a non-melting cheese, either queso fresco or añejo, is crumbled as a condiment. Quesos fresco, añejo, Oaxacan and Chihuahuan are all simple Mexican cheeses, so good and fresh in Mexico that one can only long for their flavor here. A mild French feta cheese is a good substitute for queso fresco, and parmesan or romano fills in for queso añejo. Mexican markets in the US offer some of the authentic cheeses.

Tangy crema Mexicana is drizzled as a condiment, or occasionally mixed into a sauce. Like Mexican cheese, it is a challenge to locate crema in the US. The Cacique brand available in Mexican markets is excellent. Alternatively, substitute crème fraîche, or prepare the mock crema Mexicana on page 20.

CHILES

Mexican cooking employs many different chiles. Each one contributes its own flavor and aroma to a dish, or has a particular use in Mexican cuisine. Fresh green jalapeños are used for pickles, dried red chile pequin as a condiment and fleshy poblanos are often served as stuffed vegetables. Variations in fruitiness, bite, color and other subtle flavor tones are appreciated by the chile aficionado.

The size of a chile indicates its probable heat. Small chiles are the hottest, while larger ones are milder. However, beware of the inevitable exceptions to the rule. The heat in chiles comes from the compound capsaicin, which originates not in the seeds but in the membranes. To reduce the heat of a chile, remove the membranes, and also the seeds, which sometimes pick up capsaicin from proximity. To increase the heat of a dish, add more green chile or a sprinkling of ground chile pequin. Heat aside, after cooking with this class of ingredients and tasting the results, you will learn to appreciate their many flavorful options.

DRIED CHILES

Fresh green or ripe red chiles are dried to create chiles anchos, mulatos, pasillas, guajillos, chipotles and pequin. Generally, dried chiles are tempered, soaked and puréed to create the body of richly flavored sauces. See page 17 for dried chile preparation. In some cases dried chiles, such as chipotles and pequin, are used as seasonings or condiments. When selecting dried chiles, choose pliable, untorn pods with glossy skins. Chiles anchos (often mislabeled pasillas) and mulatos are very similar in size and shape, as they originate from different varieties of fresh chile poblano. The fragrant ancho has broad 2-inch shoulders, is about 4 1/2 inches long and has wrinkled skin and a fruity flavor. The darker, slightly less-wrinkled chile mulato has a chocolatey color and flavor used to great advantage in adobo and mole sauces. The chile pasilla (also called chile negro) is dried from fresh chile chilaca. It measures 1 1/2 inches wide by 4-7 inches in length. This chile's name refers to "pasa," or raisin, due to its brown color and wrinkled skin. The shiny, wrinkle-free chile guajillo, measuring 2 inches by 4-5 inches, lends its bright red color and straightforward heat to sauces. The marvelous chile chipotle is smoked and dried—see page 41 for a detailed description. The tiny chile pequin is intensely hot and should be used in small quantities, ground as a spice.

FRESH CHILES

When selecting chiles serranos, jalapeños, Anaheims or poblanos, choose the freshest by looking for firm texture and shiny, wrinkle-free skin. Serranos are the smallest and hottest of these chiles, measuring about 1/2 inch wide and 2 inches in length. Jalapeños are the next hottest, and serve as a good substitute when serranos are unavailable. Although the serrano is hotter, the jalapeño is larger, so substitute 1/2 jalapeño for 1 serrano. The long, pale, mild Anaheim measures 1 1/2 inches wide and 5-6 inches long. Use this chile as a substitute for the chile "güero," meaning blonde, which is only available in Mexico. The Hungarian wax or banana pepper is also a good substitute for the güero. The poblano, often mistakenly called chile pasilla, is the classic choice for "chiles rellenos," or stuffed chiles. This heart-shaped chile measures 2 1/2 inches wide and 4-5 inches long, tapering to a blunt point. The bitter skins of the larger chiles must be removed before using. See page 18 for preparation instructions.

MEXICAN-STYLE CHOCOLATE ("CHOCOLATE")

Spanish explorers first experienced chocolate as a ceremonial drink served in the royal court of Montezuma. Remarkably, it took two centuries for chocolate to catch on in Europe. Today, Mexican-style chocolate refers to a composition of ground chocolate, almonds, and sugar found in the form of bars, tablets and, most recently, powder. Mexican-style chocolate is used in drinks and as an ingredient in sauces, such as mole. In Mexico, particularly in Oaxaca, the proportion of the four ingredients is so subject to personal taste that chocolate shops blend the chocolate to each patron's specifications.

"CILANTRO" (CORIANDER GREENS)

Cilantro was readily adopted into Mexican culinary practice after its introduction by Europeans. The fresh herb is sprinkled as a garnish, tossed into salads and puréed with other ingredients. Generally, only the leaves should be used, unless the herb is an ingredient in a purée.

CITRUS FRUITS

Limes and oranges were introduced into Mexico during the Spanish conquest and have become well integrated into Mexican cooking. Ceviche is one preparation that actually uses lime to "cook" seafood (see page 46). In Mexico, very small key limes are used, but the larger Persian variety makes a good substitute. The juice of Seville oranges, also called bitter oranges, is used extensively for flavoring dressings, sauces and marinades. A strange-looking fruit with dimpled, green skin, the Seville orange has a complex, bitter flavor that is difficult to replicate. See page 20 for a substitute approximating its flavor.

CLOVES ("CLAVOS")

The unopened blossoms of an evergreen tree originating in the Moluccas, or Spice Islands, cloves are frequently used in Mexican dishes. They are powerfully aromatic, so use a sparing hand—two or three cloves is usually all that is required.

CORN, HOMINY, FRESH CORN DOUGH & FLOUR ("MAÍZ," "POZOLE," "MASA" & "MASA HARINA")

Most Mexican preparations make use of some form of white field corn, which features a large kernel, little sugar and a lot of starch. The corn is dried, and later prepared by soaking the kernels with "cal," or slaked lime. This process loosens the skins, allowing them to be removed by rubbing the kernels between the hands. After removing the skin, the corn is called "nixtamal." It is then cooked whole for "pozole" (see page 20) or ground wet into fresh masa, a dough used for tortillas and tamales. Alternatively, masa harina, a flour ground from dried nixtamal, is mixed with water to form the dough. Masa harina is by no means corn meal, and the latter is not a substitute. If using masa harina, choose a good brand, such as Maseca or Quaker.

While masa harina is practical for convenient food preparation, fresh masa must be sampled to be believed. As it cooks, the incredible aroma of corn fills the air, only then allowing one to fully understand the love Mexicans have for freshly made tamales and tortillas. In the US, masa is available at tortilla factories.

CORN HUSKS ("HOJAS DE MAÍZ")

Corn husks are used throughout Mexico as wrappers for steaming food, especially tamales. See Tamales with Shredded Pork and Chile Guajillo on page 53 for instructions on how to use corn husks as tamale wrappers.

COOKING OILS & LARD ("ACEITES" & "MANTECA")

The recipes in this book generally call for mixed oil—equal parts safflower oil and good, flavorful, extra virgin olive oil. Lard is still the most commonly used cooking fat in Mexico, and traditional Mexican cooks swear by the flavor that it adds to a dish. While not authentic, mixed oil is lighter and adds a warm nuance to dishes. The olive oil infuses its flavor into food, while the safflower oil increases the smoke point, so be sure to mix them, unless called for otherwise.

CORIANDER ("SEMILLAS DE CILANTRO") & CUMIN ("COMINO")

Introduced by Europeans, coriander and cumin have taken their places as subtle enhancements to many dishes. A common mistake in American interpretations of Mexican cuisine is the addition of too much cumin. I like Diana Kennedy's apt description of the overuse as imparting a "sweaty" flavor to the dish.

"CUITLACOCHE" (CORN MUSHROOMS)

A cornfield delicacy, cuitlacoche ("wheat-la-có-chay") is a yellow-grey mushroom that develops on ears of corn. Small butterflies deposit spores on young ears, creating this rare fungus. Try Quesadillas with Chicken and Corn Mushrooms on page 68, a recipe employing the shitake mushroom and a little corn to convey, quite effectively, the delicious flavor of this freak of nature.

"EPAZOTE" (WORMSEED)

Epazote's smoky flavor is essential to the authenticity of many central and southern Mexican dishes. Mexican cooks vary radically in their opinion of whether the dried herb should be used in place of fresh. Epazote holds its flavor well when dried, and adds such a wonderful dimension to sauces that it is unthinkable not to use it. The unusual flavor and aroma soon become the subject of craving. These recipes call for the dried leaves—discard the stems.

"HOJA SANTA" (PIPER SANCTUM)

A wonderful herb for seafood, poultry, pork or beef, hoja santa is a large leaf used whole, draped over meat before wrapping it into a packet of banana leaf, parchment paper or foil. See page 58 for more descriptive information.

JAMAICA "FLOWERS" (HIBISCUS)—SEE PAGE 126 FOR A DESCRIPTION

ONIONS ("CEBOLLAS")

Unless otherwise specified, use white onions for Mexican recipes. Yellow onions commonly used in other styles of cooking are considered far too sweet.

MEXICAN OREGANO

Mexican oregano is a hot, peppery herb that retains its flavor well when dried. Oregano is always used dried in Mexican cooking, functioning more as a spice than an herb. Greek oregano has a different flavor and is not a substitute.

PUMPKIN SEEDS, SESAME SEEDS & PEANUTS ("PEPITAS," "AJONJOLI" & "CACAHUETES")

"Nueces" (nuts) and "pepitas" (seeds) are used pervasively in Mexican cooking. They are generally toasted and ground, and subsequently used to thicken sauces of Aztecan heritage. To feel instantly transported to a strange and foreign place with delicious results, try the Chicken in Green Pumpkin Seed Sauce on page 81. ◆ Shelled pumpkin seeds reveal green interior seeds known as "pepitas." Do not overbrown pepitas when toasting, or the flavor will turn unsavory. Sesame seeds decorate sweets and rolls, or create a thick foundation for many Mexican sauces. Not actually nuts, peanuts are used similarly in snacks and savory dishes.

TOMATILLOS ("TOMATES")

What a curious fruit! Actually unrelated to the tomato, the tomatillo is a member of the gooseberry family. Confusingly, it is referred to as "tomate" in Mexico, while the red tomato is called "jitomate." The flavor of tomatillos is slightly bitter and acidic, but when cooked, they make the most glorious addition to sauces, hominy stew and tamales. The freshest and most flavorful tomatillos are the small ones with completely sealed husks. Before cooking, remove the papery husk and wash the rather gummy inner surface of debris.

TOMATOES ("JITOMATES")

Tomatoes are prepared in many ways for Mexican dishes: roasted, poached, peeled or unpeeled, seeded or not, chopped, puréed or sliced. The choice is made by the cook based on tradition, the recipe or personal preference. To seed or not to seed, each decision is a considered approach to a dish. Follow the recipes to become familiar with the effects of different preparation techniques.

Preparation Techniques

(FOR DESCRIPTIONS OF THESE INGREDIENTS, SEE THE PREVIOUS SECTION)

BANANA LEAVES

To soften banana leaves for use, start by thawing the frozen packet overnight. Carefully unfold the leaves and tear pieces in the sizes specified in the recipe. Reserve extra pieces to cover tears and, if making tamales, to line the steamer. (Note: Wrap any remaining leaves and store in the refrigerator for up to a month. If mold develops, simply wipe it off before softening.) Using a moist paper towel, wipe off both sides of each leaf piece. Rinse and pat dry. Turn on a gas or electric burner to high heat. When very hot, use tongs to slowly pull each piece across the heat. The leaf will blister and pop, but do not let it burn. Turn and repeat on the other side. Set aside to cool.

DRIED CHILES

The main techniques used in preparing dried chiles are frying, to deepen the flavor, and soaking in hot water, to soften the flesh for further processing. Chiles can irritate your skin. If you are sensitive to the capsaicin, use gloves or rub vegetable oil into your fingers before handling.

Step 1. Preparing: To remove dust, wipe each chile with a moist towel. Using kitchen scissors, remove the stems and cut each chile along the sides into two flat pieces. Discard the seeds and membranes.

Step 2. Frying: In a medium skillet, heat the quantity of oil called for in the recipe over medium heat. When hot, use tongs to lay one chile piece flat in the oil. Fry for 4 seconds on each side. As the chile fries, it will stretch and lose its wrinkles a little, a sweet aroma will release and the color will become a rich tobacco hue. If the chile darkens it should be discarded, as burned chiles cause bitterness in the resulting preparation. Drain the chile on a paper towel-lined baking sheet. Reserve the chile-infused oil if called for in the recipe.

Step 3. Soaking: Place the chiles in a bowl to fit, cover with water at its boiling point and keep the chiles submerged by weighing them down with a plate. Soak for the time specified in the recipe, 30 minutes for most chiles, 45 minutes for guajillos. Oversoaking will dilute the flavor. Reserve the soaking liquid if called for in the recipe.

FRESH CHILES

Green chiles add flavor, and sometimes heat, to dishes. Chiles often vary quite a lot in heat. The normally mild poblano will sometimes be hot, and the usually hot serrano can be mild. To reduce the heat of a green chile, remove the seeds and capsaicin-laden membranes. If you are sensitive to the capsaicin, use gloves or rub vegetable oil into your fingers before handling. ◆ Larger chiles, such as Anaheims and poblanos, should have their bitter skins removed before using. The process requires roasting to char the skin, and then sweating and peeling. If making chiles rellenos, it is a good idea to roast a couple of extra chiles, just in case one doesn't make it through the process intact.

Step 1. Roasting: Preheat the broiler to 500°F and adjust the oven rack to the highest notch. Line a roasting pan with foil and place the chiles in the pan in a single layer. Roast 3 inches from the heat, turning with tongs once or twice, until well-charred, 10-15 minutes. The skins will be mostly blackened and blistered, but the flesh should not be burned. Remove from the oven.

Step 2. Sweating & Peeling: Immediately transfer the chiles to a plastic bag, seal and allow the chiles to sweat for 10 minutes. When cool, peel the skins without rinsing, which will dilute the flavor. If making rellenos, proceed to step 3. If making rajas (chile strips), skip step 3 and go to step 4.

Step 3. Preparing for Rellenos: Slit one side of the chile, leaving the stem intact. Carefully pull out the clump of seeds clinging to the inside of the stem and discard. Using a paring knife, carefully remove the remaining seeds from the chile's interior.

Step 4. Cutting "Rajas"—Chile Strips: Remove the stem, seeds and membranes, and slice each roasted and peeled chile along its length into 1/4-inch strips.

ROASTING GARLIC

Roast unpeeled garlic cloves in a skillet over medium-high heat until the skins develop brown spots and the pulp is softened, 10-15 minutes. Turn the cloves frequently to prevent burning.

ROASTING TOMATILLOS, TOMATOES & ONIONS

Roasting tomatillos, tomatoes and onions brings out their earthy quality and tremendous flavor. To start, preheat the broiler to 500°F and adjust the oven rack to the highest notch. Line a roasting pan with foil. Prepare the vegetables as required for the recipe. Remove the tomatillos' papery husks and wash. Rinse and dry the tomatoes. Leave onions unpeeled, trim the ends and cut into quarters. Place the vegetables in the pan in a single layer. Onions should have their peel facing the heat. Roast 3 inches from the heat, turning each vegetable with tongs once or twice while cooking.

Cooking time is 10-20 minutes, depending on size. When done, tomatillos will be soft and golden-green in color. Small tomatillos will be finished roasting after 10 minutes—remove them and allow larger ones to finish. Tomatoes will become soft and the cracked skins will be slightly charred. Onions are done when they are soft and the cut edges are slightly charred.

PEELING & SEEDING TOMATOES

Different choices for preparing tomatoes affect the consistency of resulting sauces. For a smoother sauce, tomatoes should be peeled, while for chunkier sauces this is unnecessary. Refer to the recipe for the required preparation.

To Peel: Peel roasted tomatoes by simply removing the loosened skin with your fingers. If the tomatoes are raw, cut out the stem and cut a small "x" on the bottom of each tomato. In a large saucepan, bring water to a boil and add the tomatoes. After 30-45 seconds, drain away the hot water and immerse the tomatoes in cold water. When cool enough to handle, peel away the split skins.

To Seed: Cut each tomato in half crosswise. Starting at the base, gently squeeze out the seeds. The motion is similar to squeezing a tube of toothpaste.

Raw spices are generally bitter, but when lightly toasted their flavors mellow and deepen. Preheat a skillet over medium-high heat. Add the spices and swirl until fragrant, 2-3 minutes. Toasted spices required for the same recipe can be processed together. If you burn the spices, do not use them. Discard and start over. ♦ Some recipes call for the spices to be ground. Use an electric spice/coffee grinder to pulverize the spices into a fine powder.

Mini-Recipes

BITTER ORANGE JUICE — YIELDS 4 TABLESPOONS

Mix I tablespoon orange juice, I tablespoon Meyer lemon or grapefruit juice and 2 tablespoons lime juice. In a pinch, use equal parts lime and orange juice.

CREMA MEXICANA — YIELDS 1/3 CUP

Whisk together 1/4 cup sour cream, I tablespoon milk and 1/8 teaspoon salt. For thinner drizzling consistency, whisk in I tablespoon milk (milder version) or I tablespoon lime juice (tangy version).

HOMINY ("POZOLE") — YIELDS 4 CUPS

Pozole, or dried white corn kernels, must be soaked in lime before preparing the stew of the same name. See the recipe for Vegetarian Hominy Stew on page 32. It takes several hours to cook the pozole, so plan accordingly.

Immerse 10 ounces of dried white field corn in cold water, remove floating kernels, drain the corn and transfer to a non-aluminum saucepan. Cover the corn with cold water 2 inches above the surface of the corn. Stir I 3/4 teaspoons of cal (slaked lime) into 1/2 cup of cold water to dissolve. Add the mixture to the corn, through a strainer if it is lumpy, and stir to mix. Bring to a simmer over medium heat, cover, reduce the heat to low and simmer until the skins easily rub off the kernels, about 20 minutes. Drain and rinse the corn, and transfer back to the pan. Submerge the corn in cold water and rub the kernels between the palms of your hands to remove the skins. Drain the corn through a sieve, allow running water to push the skins to the bottom of the sieve and remove the skins. Pick off the hard nubs from the ends of the kernels. Return the corn to the pan, cover with water 3 inches above the corn and bring the mixture to a simmer over medium-high heat. Reduce the heat to low, cover and simmer until the corn is tender, 2-4 hours depending on the age of the corn. The hominy is now ready to use in the recipe.

YUCATECAN ACHIOTE PASTE ("RECADO ROJO")

Also known as Adobo de Achiote, this seasoning paste is made of ground annatto seeds and spices. Known for its brick-red color and unique, subtle flavor, the seasoning is essential to the classic dishes from the Yucatán. Try Yucatán-Style Shredded Pork (page 64), Grilled Prawns in Achiote Citrus Marinade (page 90) or Tender Baked Fish in Banana Leaves (page 87).

YIELDS APPROXIMATELY 1/3 CUP

2 tablespoons annatto seeds

1/2 teaspoon coriander seeds, toasted

1/2 teaspoon cumin seeds, toasted

4 allspice berries, toasted

1 1/2 teaspoons dried Mexican oregano

6 whole cloves

A 1-inch piece canela

1 teaspoon black peppercorns

1 teaspoon salt

1 teaspoon masa harina

7 cloves garlic, roasted (see Techniques, page 19) and peeled

6 teaspoons cider vinegar

In a small skillet over medium-high heat, toast the annatto seeds. Remove from the heat when the seeds' color begins to transfer to the skillet, about 30 seconds. Pulverize the annatto seeds in a spice/coffee grinder, rocking the grinder upside down repeatedly for 3 minutes. Take the time to grind the seeds into a very fine powder—when finished, the powder will be fine enough to cling to the lid of the grinder. Transfer the powder to a small dish. Pulverize the coriander, cumin, allspice, oregano, cloves, canela and peppercorns. Mix the ground spices, salt and masa harina into the annatto powder and set aside. Using a fork, mash the garlic into a paste on a flat surface. Sprinkle a little spice powder over the garlic. Press and scrape the garlic and spices together. Add a teaspoon of the vinegar and work it in with the fork. Mix in the rest of the powder and vinegar incrementally until a thick, pliable paste is formed. Transfer the paste to a small bowl or jar. Cover and let the flavors develop for at least 1 hour, or preferably overnight.

CHILE ADOBO MARINADE ("ADOBO")

Most of the world's cultures have made the discovery that salt preserves meat. However, the combination of chile and salt acting as a preservative is distinctly Mexican. Particulars of the adobo recipe vary across Mexico, but the end result is always delicious. Try the Roast Pork Loin in Adobo (page 72).

YIELDS 3/4 CUP

2 tablespoons mixed oil (see page 15)

3 chiles guajillos, fried (see Techniques, page 17)

2 chiles anchos, fried (see Techniques, page 17)

4 cloves garlic, roasted (see Techniques, page 19), peeled and coarsely chopped

1/2 small white onion, peeled and coarsely chopped

1/4 teaspoon cumin seeds, toasted

7 whole cloves

A 1/2-inch piece canela

1/4 teaspoon dried thyme

1/4 teaspoon dried Mexican oregano

1 teaspoon salt

5 tablespoons bitter orange juice (page 20)

Using the oil, prepare the chiles as instructed in Techniques and reserve the oil in the skillet. Soak the chiles for 45 minutes. Transfer the roasted garlic to a blender. Reheat the chile skillet and oil over medium-high heat. When hot, sauté the onion until it browns, about 5 minutes, and add to the blender. In a spice/coffee grinder, pulverize the cumin, cloves and canela into a powder. Add to the blender along with the thyme, oregano, salt and bitter orange juice. Drain the chiles, transfer to the blender, and purée. The sauce will keep in a covered jar in the refrigerator for up to a week. For very lengthy storage, omit the bitter orange juice until ready to use the adobo marinade.

Soups, Salads, Relishes & Salsas

Light Chicken Broth

CALDO DE POLLO

A good light broth is essential to making a flavorful Mexican sauce, or tasty tamale dough. A whole chicken breast is used in this recipe, providing meat for Shredded Chicken (see below) and some bone to flavor the broth. Although heavy European-style stocks are fabulous for soups, they dominate the flavors in a Mexican sauce, and a light broth is preferred. Homemade broth also has the advantage of excluding the MSG and excessive salt often found in canned stocks. However, when short on time, dilute 4 cups of canned stock with 2 cups of water. If you wish, simmer some of the vegetables below with the diluted canned stock for a fresher taste.

YIELDS 6 1/2 CUPS

1/4 teaspoon dried marjoram

1/4 teaspoon dried thyme

1/2 teaspoon dried Mexican oregano

8 black peppercorns, cracked (pulse twice in a spice/coffee grinder)

1 bay leaf, torn into large pieces

1 tablespoon mixed oil (see page 15)

1/2 white onion, peeled and roughly chopped

2 cloves garlic, unpeeled and crushed with a mallet or the side of a knife

1/2 large or 1 small carrot, peeled and cut into 1-inch pieces

2 small stalks celery with light green leaves, cut into 1-inch pieces

1 large whole chicken breast (about 1 1/4 pounds), with skin and center keel bone

3/4 teaspoon salt

Prepare the marjoram, thyme, oregano, peppercorns and bay leaf in a bouquet garni (see Cooking Notes below). Heat the oil in a large stockpot over medium-high heat. When hot, add the onion, garlic, carrot and celery. Sauté until the onion becomes translucent, about 5 minutes. Add the bouquet garni and lay the whole chicken breast over the mixture. Cover the chicken with 8 cups of cold water. When the mixture begins to simmer, reduce the heat to very low and continue to simmer, partially covered, until the chicken is barely cooked and tender, 20-25 minutes. Remove the chicken from the broth with tongs and let it cool long enough to be handled, about 10 minutes. Remove the skin and discard. Remove the meat from the bones and set aside to be shredded (see below). Crack the rib bones. Discard the cartilage from the center keel bone and chop the bone into 4 pieces with a meat cleaver. Add the bones back to the pot. Continue to simmer the broth, partially covered, for 1 1/2 hours, skimming the surface of foam after 5-10 minutes. Strain the broth through a sieve and allow to cool. Cover and refrigerate. Remove any congealed fat from the surface before using. Unused broth may be frozen in 2 cup quantities for future use.

Cooking Notes

Preparing a Bouquet Garni: In Mexico, a bouquet garni is called "una muñeca," or a little doll. This cheesecloth bundle encloses spices and herbs, allowing easy removal from the broth. Cut a 3-inch square of cheesecloth and place the herbs and spices in the center. Bring the corners up and cinch the packet around the spices with a piece of string, or tie the corners to create a miniature satchel.

Shredded Chicken

POLLO DESHEBRADO

YIELDS 2 CUPS

The preceding Light Chicken Broth recipe saves time by preparing both broth and shredded chicken at the same time. Usually the chicken is poached in pre-made broth and allowed to cool in it, providing the meat with greater flavor. Try this if you have the time, or, in a pinch, poach the chicken in diluted canned stock. In either case, use enough liquid to cover the meat and simmer for 20 minutes.

To shred the meat, pull it apart with your fingers along the grain into pieces about 1/4 inch thick and 2 inches long. The meat may be wrapped tightly and frozen.

Fennel & Leek Vegetable Broth

CALDO DE VERDURAS

Unbelievably delicious and slightly piquant, this broth is designed to be a little more full-flavored than Light Chicken Broth (page 24), adding a delightful dimension to vegetarian stews and fillings. Keep in mind that the freshest ingredients will result in a richly flavored broth, and the extra effort to make it will pay in spades as your family and guests devour their meals. This broth smells divine as it cooks too. Use the broth in Pueblan Five Vegetable Green Mole (page 96), Vegetarian Hominy Stew (page 32) or in vegetarian versions of many recipes in this book.

YIELDS 8 CUPS

2 tablespoons mixed oil (see page 15)

1 white onion, unpeeled and halved

2 cloves garlic, unpeeled and crushed with a mallet or the side of a knife

2 large leeks, trimmed, both white and green parts cut into 1-inch pieces

2 carrots, peeled and cut into 1-inch pieces

2 stalks celery, cut into 1-inch pieces

1 small fennel bulb with fronds, cut into 1/4-inch slices

6 sprigs fresh flat-leaf parsley

1 teaspoon dried thyme

3 bay leaves, torn into large pieces

1/2 teaspoon black peppercorns, cracked (pulse twice in a spice/coffee grinder)

1 chile jalapeño, quartered lengthwise

1 teaspoon salt

In a large, thick-sided saucepan, heat the oil over medium-high heat. When hot, add the onion halves, cut side down, and cook until the cut sides have blackened, about 5 minutes. Reduce the heat to medium and add the garlic, leeks, carrots, celery and fennel. Sauté until the vegetables wilt and brighten in color, about 10 minutes. Add all of the remaining ingredients and 10 cups of cold water. Bring the mixture to a boil over high heat, reduce the heat to a low simmer, partially cover and cook for 1 hour.

Immediately strain the broth through a fine wire mesh sieve, or a colander with a couple of layers of cheesecloth. Press on the solids to remove as much of the liquid as possible. Transfer to a storage container, allow to cool and skim. Keep the broth in the refrigerator for up to 5 days, or transfer to storage bags in 2 cup quantities and freeze for future use.

A FEATHERED SERPENT TRAVELLING OVER
SEASHELLS, THE AZTEC GODDESS QUETZALCÓATL
IS A BEAUTIFUL METAPHOR FOR THE
REGENERATIVE FORCE OF LIFE.
TENOCHTITLÁN.

Rustic Black Bean Soup

SOPA DE FRIJOLES CHARROS

"Charros" are the colorful cowboys of the northern Mexican ranchos. The use of the word charros generally implies rustic, and that is the nature of this soup. It is easy to imagine a nice cup of it after a rigorous day of cattle herding, but in fact, this recipe was described after a not-so-rigorous day of beach chair-sitting at Villa del Sol in Zihuatenejo. It is made of nutritionally substantial black beans, and has a great, hearty flavor that perfectly satisfies true hunger. Serve the soup steaming hot after skiing, or any vigorous weekend activity.

SERVES 4 TO 6 ♦ YIELDS 5 CUPS

2 tablespoons mixed oil (see page 15)

1/3 white onion, peeled and minced

2 teaspoons dried epazote (leaves only)

1/2 cup black beans, rinsed and picked over for stones and split beans

1/4 teaspoon cumin seeds, toasted

2 whole cloves

A 3/8-inch piece canela

2 cloves garlic, peeled and minced

2 1/2 chiles serranos (about 2 inches each), stemmed, quartered lengthwise, seeds and membranes removed, minced

1 chorizo sausage, minced

2 plum tomatoes, seeded (see Techniques, page 19) and finely chopped

4 teaspoons rice vinegar

1 teaspoon salt, or to taste

1/4 teaspoon freshly ground black pepper

Garnish:

1 1/2 limes, quartered

4-6 teaspoons crema Mexicana (page 20), drizzling consistency, or cream (optional)

2 tablespoons fresh cilantro (leaves only)

In a large, thick-sided saucepan, heat 1 tablespoon of the oil over medium-high heat. When hot, add 2 tablespoons of the minced onion and sauté until translucent, about 4 minutes. Stir in the epazote. Add the rinsed beans and 4 cups of cold water, stir once or twice and bring to a simmer. Reduce the heat to low and continue to simmer until the skins of the beans have softened, 40-50 minutes.

While the beans are cooking, prepare the other ingredients. In a spice/coffee grinder, pulverize the cumin, cloves and canela into a fine powder. Set the spices aside in a small dish. Heat the remaining 1 tablespoon of oil in a medium skillet over medium-high heat. When hot, add the remaining onion and sauté just until it begins to brown, about 5 minutes. Add the garlic, chiles and ground spices. Stir to mix and sauté until the chiles turn bright green, about 2 minutes. Add the chorizo and sauté until it browns, about 4 minutes. Add the tomatoes and cook until they have softened and much of their juice has cooked away, about 5 minutes. Set aside.

When the beans have completed their initial cooking, add the sausage mixture, reserving the sausage skillet for de-glazing. Add 2 cups of cold water to the beans and stir to mix. Reheat the sausage skillet over medium-high heat. When hot, add the vinegar. De-glaze the pan by loosening and scraping the brownings from the pan. Transfer the resulting liquid to the beans, stir to mix and continue simmering the soup until the beans have softened, but are not mushy, 40-60 minutes. The beans should not be too soft, nor should they be al dente—hard to the tooth. Add the salt and pepper. Taste for balance of flavor, adding a pinch more salt or a dash of vinegar if necessary—the correct balance of salt and vinegar will give the soup a savory and bright flavor. To serve, spoon the soup into small bowls, squeeze a piece of lime over each bowl, drizzle the optional cream on the surface and top with cilantro leaves.

Chicken Soup With Lime & Tortilla Strips

SOPA DE LIMA

Chicken soup is found the world over. The addition of lime juice, herbs and spices makes Mexico's version both light and heartwarming. The components of this soup are attractively assembled in each bowl and the broth is added to create little tomato and cilantro topped islands. This mode of presentation gives an uncommonly pretty appearance to the soup, and leaves the ingredients crisp in texture and fresh in taste. To live up to the soup's name, squeeze additional lime juice over the top with abandon. Tiny, sour key limes are used for this soup in Mexico, but our Persian limes work just fine.

SERVES 4

4 corn tortillas, laid out to dry

1 tablespoon extra virgin olive oil

4 1/2 cups light chicken broth (page 24)

1/4-1/2 teaspoon salt, to taste

1 1/2 cups shredded chicken (page 25)

1 chile jalapeño, stem, seeds and membranes removed, minced

1/2 small red onion, peeled and sliced into thin half moons, cut again into quarters

2 plum tomatoes, seeded (see Techniques, page 19) and finely chopped

1/2 cup fresh cilantro (leaves only), coarsely chopped

3 limes, preferably key limes, quartered

Preheat the oven to 450°F. Brush both sides of each tortilla with the oil and place the tortillas in a stack. Cut the tortillas in half, then slice crosswise into 1/4-inch strips. Place the tortilla strips on a baking sheet in a single layer and bake until crisp, about 10 minutes. Set aside.

Heat the broth and add the salt, if necessary. If the broth is unsalted, you may need to add more salt than indicated. While the broth is heating, evenly divide the chicken into individual soup bowls. Top the chicken with a generous amount of baked tortilla strips, reserving 1/2 cup for garnish. On top of the chips, arrange 1/2-1 teaspoon minced chile, 1 tablespoon onion, 1 tablespoon tomato and a sprinkling of cilantro in each bowl. Transfer the remaining quantities of each vegetable to a small serving platter along with the reserved tortilla strips. Ladle the heated broth into the bowls until most, but not all, of the composed ingredients are covered. They should appear as little islands, with the tomato and cilantro showing off their colors at the top. Squeeze 2 lime quarters over each serving and discard the rinds. Place the remaining lime quarters on the platter with the vegetables and tortilla strips. Serve the soup and pass the platter to your diners for their garnishing pleasure as the soup is eaten.

Vegetarian Hominy Stew

POZOLE VERDE VEGETARIANA

Contrary to popular belief, vegetarian dishes are commonly found in Mexican home cooking. Not only are vegetables nutritious and economical, those in Mexico are particularly tasty due to the perpetuation of "criollo" farming (see page 10). This hearty hominy preparation features a delicious, mushroom-enhanced broth that is wonderful on a cold, rainy night. Pozole should be served with its traditional condiments, which add a bright, raw note to the earthy, long-simmered flavor of the stew.

SERVES 8

For Advance Preparation

4 cups hominy (page 20) plus 1 cup of its liquid, or a 29-ounce can hominy, drained, plus 1 cup broth or water

For the Pozole

1/2 pound button mushrooms, trimmed and quartered

1/4 pound oyster mushrooms, trimmed and sliced

3 cups vegetable or light chicken broth (page 26 or 24)

3/4 pound tomatillos (about 13 small to medium), husks removed and washed

4 cloves garlic, unpeeled

1/2 white onion, unpeeled and halved

1-2 chiles serranos, stemmed and cut into thirds crosswise

3/4 cup fresh cilantro, loosely packed

4 tablespoons pepitas (green pumpkin seeds), unsalted

2 tablespoons sesame seeds

2 whole cloves

A 1/2-inch piece canela

1/2 teaspoon black peppercorns

2 tablespoons mixed oil (see page 15)

1 tablespoon dried epazote (leaves only), crumbled

1 teaspoon salt, or to taste

Condiments:

3/4 cup white onion, peeled and cut into 1/4-inch cubes

3/4 cup fresh cilantro (leaves only), coarsely chopped

3 red radishes, thinly sliced

2 limes, quartered

In a large saucepan, combine the mushrooms and broth and bring to a simmer over medium-high heat. Reduce the heat to low, cover and cook until the mushrooms are tender, about 5 minutes. Set aside to cool. Drain the mushrooms, reserving the broth. Set aside both the broth and the mushrooms.

Preheat the broiler to 500°F. Line a roasting pan with foil and place the tomatillos, garlic and onion, peel facing upward, in the pan. Roast until softened, about 15 minutes. Peel the garlic and onion, and transfer to a blender. Add the roasted tomatillos, chiles and cilantro and coarsely purée, being careful not to overblend. Set aside.

In a small skillet over medium-high heat, toast the pepitas until they swell and crackle, about 3 minutes. Do not let them brown. Transfer to a spice/coffee grinder. Toast the sesame seeds until they are light brown, 2-3 minutes, and transfer them to the grinder. Add the cloves, canela and peppercorns to the grinder and pulverize into a fine powder.

In a thick-sided saucepan or Dutch oven, heat the oil over medium-high heat. When hot, add the tomatillo purée and the seed/spice powder. Stir and sauté the purée until it bubbles and thickens, about 5 minutes. Add the mushroom broth, mushrooms, epazote, hominy and its liquid, and bring to a simmer. Reduce the heat to low, cover and simmer until thickened into a creamy consistency, about 40 minutes. If it is too thick, stir in more liquid. If too thin, allow the mixture to simmer for 10 more minutes uncovered. Stir in the salt.

Spoon the pozole into small bowls and sprinkle some onion, cilantro and radishes on top. Squeeze a lime quarter over each portion and serve hot. Place extra condiments in small bowls to be added at whim.

Jicama, Pineapple & Watercress Salad

ENSALADA DE JÍCAMA Y PIÑA

Jicama has a wonderful crunch and subtle, sweet flavor, making it a welcome addition to salads. Sweet pineapple and tart watercress combine refreshingly with the jicama to complement seafood, poultry, pork or anything else. This salad is a perfect course in a backyard picnic menu including Lime Marinated Scallop Cocktail (page 46) and Black Bean and Corn Salsa (page 40).

SERVES 4 TO 6

9 ounces jicama, peeled and cut into matchsticks (about 2 cups)

4 tablespoons bitter orange juice (page 20)

2 tablespoons extra virgin olive oil

1/2 teaspoon freshly ground black pepper

3/8 teaspoon salt

1/8-1/4 teaspoon chile pequin

2 tablespoons peanuts, unskinned and unsalted

2-3 bunches watercress, washed and stems trimmed

2/3 cup fresh pineapple, or canned sliced pineapple, cut into 1/2-inch cubes

In a medium bowl, combine the jicama and 2 tablespoons of the bitter orange juice and set aside for 15 minutes. In a small bowl, whisk the remaining 2 tablespoons bitter orange juice with the oil, pepper and salt. Set aside. In a small skillet over medium-high heat, toast the chiles for 30 seconds and transfer them to a spice/coffee grinder. Toast the peanuts until fragrant, about 3 minutes, and transfer to the grinder. Pulse to coarsely chop and set aside.

Drain the jicama and combine it in a serving bowl with the watercress and pineapple. Pour the bitter orange juice and olive oil dressing over the salad. Toss to coat, sprinkle with the ground chile and peanuts and toss again. Serve.

Pickled Red Onions

CEBOLLAS EN ESCABECHE

The fresh pickle taste and pink color of these onions make them a popular item to keep around the house for a variety of meals, Mexican or not. They will keep in the refrigerator for up to a month, and are especially good with the pibils of the Yucatán (pages 64 and 87).

YIELDS 2 CUPS

1 red onion, peeled and sliced into 1/8-inch thick half moons

3/4 teaspoon salt

2 tablespoons mixed oil (see page 15)

4 allspice berries

3/4 teaspoon dried Mexican oregano

1-2 bay leaves

4 tablespoons mild vinegar, such as rice or sherry vinegar

2 tablespoons bitter orange juice (page 20)

3/8 teaspoon sugar

1/4 teaspoon freshly ground black pepper

Place the onions in a bowl and cover them with cold water. Sprinkle with 1/2 teaspoon of the salt and mix with your hand. Let the onions stand for 10 minutes. Drain well in a colander.

Heat the oil in a medium skillet over medium heat. When hot, add the onions, allspice, oregano and bay leaves. Stir to mix and sauté until the onions are tender and slightly wilted, but not brown, about 3 minutes. Remove from the heat and transfer to a bowl. Mix in the vinegar, bitter orange juice, sugar, pepper and the remaining salt. Taste for balance of flavor—the sweet and salt flavors should register evenly on your tongue. If the mixture is too sweet, add another large pinch of salt and mix. Place the onions in the refrigerator to macerate for at least 15 minutes before serving.

Pickled Jalapeños

Homemade pickled chiles are, of course, much more flavorful than the canned variety. Not only a relish, pickled chiles and their juice are used as ingredients in many recipes. Veracruz-Style Red Snapper with Olives and Chiles (page 84) is one such delicious dish, in which the pickle juice gives a distinguishing touch to the sauce. If the chiles are to be used as a table condiment, the heat may be reduced considerably by removing the seeds and membranes before pickling. Make the pickles a day in advance for the best flavor.

YIELDS 1 TO 1 1/2 CUPS

2 tablespoons safflower oil

2-3 cloves garlic, peeled and halved

1/3 white onion, peeled and cut into thin half moons

1/2 large carrot, peeled and cut into 1/8-inch diagonal slices

1/4 pound chiles jalapeños (about 6-8 chiles) with stems, sliced in half lengthwise

1/4 teaspoon cumin seeds

1 whole clove

1/8 teaspoon black peppercorns

1/4 teaspoon dried thyme

1/2 teaspoon dried Mexican oregano

2 bay leaves

2 tablespoons mild vinegar, such as rice or sherry vinegar

6 tablespoons cider vinegar

1 teaspoon brown sugar

1/4 teaspoon salt

In a medium skillet, heat the oil over medium heat. When hot, add the garlic, onion, carrot and chiles. Sauté until the onion softens, but is not brown, about 4 minutes. In a spice/coffee grinder, pulverize the cumin, clove and peppercorns, rocking the grinder upside down repeatedly. Transfer the spices to the cooking chiles. Add the thyme, oregano and bay leaves, 1/2 cup of cold water, the vinegars, brown sugar and salt, and stir to combine. Raise the heat to medium-high and bring the mixture to a boil. Reduce the heat to low, cover and simmer until the chiles are an olive color and the carrots are a little soft, 8-10 minutes. Set aside to cool. Transfer the chiles and juice to a non-metallic storage container, cover and store overnight before using. They will keep indefinitely in the refrigerator.

IN OAXACA, TWO
PAPIER MÂCHÉ SKELETONS AND A
SAND PAINTING ADORN
THE CATHEDRAL ENTRANCE FOR
THE DAYS OF THE DEAD,
NOVEMBER 1 AND 2.

Pickled Green Cabbage Relish

COL EN ESCABECHE

This tasty relish adds a bright, crisp quality to meals that include tortilla and masa preparations. It is especially good with the delicious Enchiladas with Chile Sauce (page 60). For the best flavor, allow the cabbage to marinate overnight.

YIELDS 4 CUPS

1/2 cup rice vinegar

1 tablespoon extra virgin olive oil

1 teaspoon dried Mexican oregano

1 bay leaf, torn into thirds

1/8-1/4 teaspoon chile pequin, pulverized in a spice/coffee grinder

1 teaspoon sugar

1/4 teaspoon freshly ground black pepper

1/4 teaspoon salt

1 medium carrot, peeled and grated (about 1/2 cup)

1/4 white onion, peeled and minced

1/2 green cabbage, shredded (see Cooking Notes below), about 4 cups

Place all of the ingredients except the cabbage in a small bowl. Whisk to combine well and set aside. Place the cabbage in a large bowl. Pour the vinegar mixture over the top of the cabbage and toss with your hands to mix well. If using the same day, let the cabbage marinate for at least 1 hour at room temperature. For even better flavor, marinate overnight in the refrigerator.

Cooking Notes

Shredding Cabbage: Core and quarter the cabbage lengthwise. Cut very thin ribbon-like slices along the length. Do not use a grater—grated cabbage throws off too much water during marination, making for an unappealing presentation.

Guacamole

Guacamole is a tasty and familiar relish, easily adapted for different uses. A chunky-style guacamole, made with chopped tomato, cilantro and white onion, stands up to dipping, while a thin sauce puréed with water, cilantro and chiles is great for drizzling over tacos or tostadas (pages 62-66). This simple recipe highlights the fresh flavor of the avocados. Taste as you add the minced chile until reaching your preferred Scoville rating. Serve in a small bowl with chips, or as a relish alongside a meal. The color will stay fresh for about an hour, so prepare this dish shortly before serving. If you are worried about the avocado browning, generously squeeze lime juice over the top and stir it in right before serving.

YIELDS 3 CUPS

3 Hass avocados, ripe

3-5 chiles serranos (about 2 inches each), stemmed, quartered lengthwise, seeds and membranes removed, minced

1/4 teaspoon freshly ground black pepper

1/4 teaspoon salt, or to taste

Cut each avocado in half lengthwise, turning the knife around the pit. Pull the avocado apart—the pit will probably remain in one half. Firmly and carefully hit the avocado pit with the sharp edge of the knife to wedge it in the pit. Turn and wiggle the knife to lift out the pit, and discard. Holding an avocado half in one hand, use the knife to crosshatch the flesh, but not the skin. Scoop out the flesh with a spoon, or run your thumb between the skin and the pulp, lifting the chunks out and into a bowl.

Mash the avocado with a fork until it is just a little lumpy. Add 4-6 tablespoons of water, continuing to mash and stir in water until the mixture is a thick, coarse purée. Add the chiles, pepper and salt. Taste for balance of flavor, making adjustments as desired.

Black Bean & Corn Salsa

SALSA DE FRIJOLES Y ELOTE

More like a relish or salad, this salsa may be served as a sassy side dish. You may also make creative use of it in tostadas, in tacos or as an accompaniment to chips and guacamole (page 39). If presentation is important for a special occasion, place the beans in a sieve and gently rinse to prevent a muddy effect on the corn and other ingredients. Unfortunately, this will also remove a bit of the bean flavor, so if taste is the key pursuit, drain the beans but don't rinse them.

SERVES 6

1 cup Oaxacan-Style Beans in Broth (page 115), or canned black beans, drained

1 large ear corn, parboiled and kernels cut from the cob (see Cooking Notes, page 49)

1/4 small white onion, peeled and finely chopped

1 1/2 plum tomatoes, seeded (see Techniques, page 19) and finely chopped

5 tablespoons fresh cilantro (leaves only), coarsely chopped

1 chile serrano, stemmed, quartered lengthwise, seeds and membranes removed, minced

4 teaspoons rice vinegar

1 tablespoon extra virgin olive oil

1/4 teaspoon freshly ground black pepper

1/4 teaspoon salt

1/2-1 lime, quartered

In a medium bowl, combine all of the ingredients except the lime and mix well. Squeeze half the lime over the top and mix again. Taste for balance of flavor, and add more lime juice, vinegar or salt, if necessary. Serve chilled.

Chipotle Salsa

"Chipotle" is derived from the Nuahatl word meaning smoked chile. During the chile harvest, many varieties of jalapeño are smoked over slow-burning fires. The tan chile chipotle with small, dark brown stripes is made from a fresh green jalapeño. The chile morita is also chile chipotle, but is made from a small variety of jalapeño allowed to ripen to a red color. Each smoked chile has its nuance of flavor, but whatever the variety, all chipotles add the unforgettable flavor combination of smoke, heat and chile-chocolate overtones to condiments and other dishes. Try this salsa in Masa Boats with Corn and Zucchini Filling (page 47) or on Roasted Beef Tenderloin (page 76). A smidgen on a hot corn tortilla with beans and a sprinkling of cheese is simple to prepare and also delicious.

YIELDS 1/2 CUP

2 chiles chipotles, stems, seeds and membranes removed

2 plum tomatoes

3 large cloves garlic, unpeeled

1 small white onion, unpeeled and quartered

1 tablespoon safflower oil

1/4 teaspoon salt, or to taste

Place the chipotles in a small bowl and cover with water at its boiling point. Soak the chiles for 30 minutes. Preheat the broiler to 400°F, with the oven rack on the second-to-highest notch. Line a roasting pan with foil and place the tomatoes, garlic and onion, peel facing upward, in the pan. Roast until the garlic is soft and the tomatoes are cooked through, 20-30 minutes. Remove the peels and any hardened areas from the garlic and onion. Transfer, along with the tomatoes, to a blender. Drain the chiles, reserving 1/2 cup of the soaking liquid, and add both to the blender. Purée. Heat the oil in a small skillet over medium heat. When hot, add the purée and sauté until it thickens and the color deepens, 10-15 minutes. Add the salt. Cover and store in the refrigerator.

Fresh Tomato Salsa

SALSA MEXICANA OR PICO DE GALLO

When tomatoes are at their peak of ripeness, there is no better use for them than this salsa. Serve as an accompaniment to almost anything, from chips and tacos, to grilled fish and roasted meats. Try it with Little Black Bean and Corn Cakes (page 50). The salsa is simple to prepare and a tasty, colorful delight on the table.

YIELDS 2 CUPS

6 plum tomatoes, seeded (see Techniques, page 19) and finely chopped

1/4 small white onion, peeled and minced

1 chile jalapeño, stem, seeds and membranes removed, minced

1 tablespoon fresh lime juice

2 tablespoons fresh cilantro (leaves only), minced

1/2 teaspoon fresh mint leaves, minced

1/2 teaspoon salt

1/8 teaspoon rice vinegar (optional)

In a small bowl, combine all of the ingredients except the vinegar, stir to mix and taste for salt. If the tomatoes are winter tomatoes and lack sweetness, add the vinegar. Allow the flavors to combine for 30 minutes at room temperature before serving.

Roasted Tomatillo Salsa

SALSA VERDE ASADA

The tomatillo is a unique fruit, a member of the gooseberry family. It is used in savory dishes, much like the tomato. Tomatillos add their own unique flavor profile to traditional Mexican cooking, and green tomatoes are in no way a substitute. Serve this versatile salsa with tortilla chips, quesadillas, tacos, Masa Boats with Corn and Zucchini Filling (page 47) or Roasted Beef Tenderloin (page 76).

YIELDS 2 CUPS

1 pound tomatillos (about 18 small to medium), roasted (see Techniques, page 19)

12 cloves garlic, roasted (see Techniques, page 19) and peeled

1-2 chiles jalapeños, stems removed and minced (with seeds and membranes)

1/2 cup fresh cilantro (leaves only), coarsely chopped

1/4 teaspoon salt

Transfer the roasted tomatillos and the liquid from the roasting pan to a bowl and allow to cool. When cool enough to handle, coarsely chop the tomatillos and transfer them back to the bowl with any liquid from the cutting board. Coarsely mash the roasted garlic on a cutting board with the back of a fork and add to the tomatillos. Add the chiles, cilantro and salt. Stir to combine and taste for salt. Cover and store the salsa in the refrigerator for up to 3 days.

Cooked Green Salsa

Most Americans eat salsa—in fact, it is beating ketchup in the condiment popularity polls. We generally think of salsa as Fresh Tomato Salsa (page 42), freshly chopped garden tomatoes with green chiles, so famously combined with tortilla chips. However delicious, Fresh Tomato Salsa is not simmered to combine its flavors, so it is often referred to in Mexico as "the lazy woman's salsa." Cooked Green Salsa is an example of a simmered salsa. It makes its appearance throughout Mexico in a variety of recipes. Try it in Chicken Tamales Flavored with Fennel Greens (page 56), or simply serve it with chips.

YIELDS 1 CUP

3/4 pound tomatillos (about 13 small to medium), husks removed and washed

2 cloves garlic, peeled and coarsely chopped

1/8 white onion, peeled and coarsely chopped

2 1/2 chiles serranos (about 2 inches each), stems, seeds and membranes removed

2 tablespoons fresh cilantro, coarsely chopped

1 tablespoon safflower oil

1/4 teaspoon freshly ground black pepper, or to taste

1/2 teaspoon salt, or to taste

In a medium saucepan, arrange the tomatillos in a single layer. Barely cover the tomatillos with water. Bring to a boil over medium-high heat. Reduce the heat to low and cook the tomatillos until they are soft, 12-15 minutes. Drain the tomatillos, reserving 1/4 cup of the poaching liquid. Transfer the garlic, onion, chiles, cilantro, tomatillos and reserved poaching liquid to a blender. Purée until smooth. In a medium skillet, heat the oil over medium-high heat. When very hot, add the purée and sauté until it is reduced by 1/3, 10-15 minutes. The color will be bright green. Stir in the pepper and salt to taste.

Antojitos, First Courses & Masa Treats

Lime Marinated Scallop Cocktail

C E V I C H E

Lime juice alone is used to cook the scallops in this traditional coastal Mexican dish. The thinly sliced scallops and colorful fresh vegetables create a texture and flavor which is positively sublime. For a seafood lovers' menu, this ceviche makes a light and refreshing appetizer followed by Veracruz-Style Red Snapper with Olives and Chiles (page 84) and Arroz Blanco (page 110).

S E R V E S   6

1/2 pound sea scallops, cut into 1/8-inch thick slices

3/4 cup fresh lime juice (about 3-6 limes)

4 teaspoons extra virgin olive oil

1/4 teaspoon freshly ground black pepper

1/2 teaspoon salt

4 tablespoons yellow bell pepper, stem, seeds and membranes removed, finely chopped

1 1/2 cups cherry tomatoes, sliced in half and seeds squeezed out

2 chiles serranos, stemmed, quartered lengthwise, seeds and membranes removed, minced

4 tablespoons red onion, peeled and finely chopped

1/2 avocado, peeled and cut into 1/4-inch cubes (about 4 tablespoons)

1/2 teaspoon fresh mint leaves, minced

2 tablespoons fresh cilantro (leaves only), coarsely chopped

Garnish: Paper-thin sliced radishes, fresh cilantro leaves and lime wedges

In a non-metallic bowl, stir to coat the scallops with the lime juice. Cover and refrigerate until the scallops are opaque throughout, about 30 minutes. Drain the scallops through a sieve and transfer to a medium bowl. Toss gently with the remaining ingredients and taste for balance of flavor. Place each serving on a butter lettuce leaf or in a margarita glass. Top with a few sliced radishes, cilantro leaves and a squeeze of lime. Serve chilled.

Masa Boats With Corn & Zucchini Filling

SOPES CON ELOTE Y CALABACITAS

"Antojitos," or little whims, are masa snacks. Tacos, enchiladas and anything made with a tortilla fall into this category, but sopes are the true essence of an antojito. The crispy masa shells are loaded with a variety of fillings and toppings. Popped into the mouth, they are simply irresistible packets of flavor. Sopes also make a visually tantalizing appetizer. After the preparation is done, they are relatively quick to pull together, allowing them to be served hot with little effort. The filling may be prepared a day in advance, and the sope shells baked 1-2 hours before assembly.

SERVES 6 TO 10 ♦ YIELDS 20 SOPES

For Sope Assembly

1/2 cup drained Beans in Broth (page 114), preferably without aniseed, plus 2 tablespoons of bean broth, puréed together in a blender

1 recipe Chipotle Salsa (page 41) and/or Roasted Tomatillo Salsa (page 43)

4 romaine lettuce leaves, cut crosswise into 1/8-inch ribbons (optional)

1/3 cup crema Mexicana (page 20), drizzling consistency (optional)

1/3 cup queso fresco, or mild feta cheese, crumbled

For the Corn and Zucchini Filling

1 tablespoon mixed oil (see page 15)

1/2 white onion, peeled and chopped into 1/4-inch cubes

2 cloves garlic, peeled and minced

2 small zucchini, trimmed and cut into 1/4-inch cubes

1 ear corn, parboiled and kernels cut from the cob (see Cooking Notes below)

2 teaspoons dried epazote (leaves only)

1/2 teaspoon dried Mexican oregano

1/4 cup queso fresco, or mild feta cheese, crumbled

Preparing the Filling: In a medium skillet, heat the oil over medium-high heat. When hot, add the onion and sauté until it begins to brown, about 5 minutes. Add the garlic and sauté for 2 minutes. Add the zucchini and sauté until it begins to soften, about 3 minutes. Add the corn, epazote and oregano and cook another 2 minutes. Stir in the cheese and remove from the heat. Set aside for sope assembly, or cool and store in the refrigerator.

For the Sope Shells
3/4 cup masa harina
1/4 teaspoon salt
1/2 teaspoon baking powder
1/2 cup very warm water
3 tablespoons extra virgin olive oil

Preparing the Sope Shells: In a small bowl, combine the masa harina, salt and baking powder. Add the water and use your hands to mix into a smooth dough. Add 1 tablespoon of the oil and knead until well mixed. Cover with a damp towel and let stand for 30 minutes.

Check the consistency of the dough—it should be very pliable and slightly tacky. If the dough is dry, work in very warm water a teaspoon at a time until the correct consistency is achieved. If the dough is sticky, work in a teaspoon of masa harina. Form the dough into 10 balls, about 1 1/2 inches in diameter. Keep the dough balls covered with a towel. One at a time, gently press each ball with the flattened palm of your hand until it becomes a thick wafer, 3/8 inch thick and 2 inches in diameter. Heat a large, thick-bottomed skillet over medium-high heat. Do not add oil. When the skillet is hot, add 5 wafers in a single layer and cook until slightly browned, 2-3 minutes. Flip and cook for another 2-3 minutes. The inner dough will still be soft. Transfer the wafers to a plate, cover and set aside until cool enough to handle.

Preheat the oven to 350°F. Using a narrow blade, such as a steak knife, cut the wafer apart, forming 2 thin disks. Place the cooked side down on a work surface and push the uncooked dough out from the center to form a pinched edge. This is your sope shell, or masa boat. Place it on a baking sheet and loosely cover. Repeat the process for all the halved wafers. Brush the sope shells with the remaining 2 tablespoons of oil and bake until light golden brown, about 15 minutes. If not assembling immediately, cool the sope shells slightly to prevent sogginess, then cover tightly until ready to assemble.

Assembling the Sopes: If necessary, reheat the sope shells, uncovered, in a pre-heated 200°F oven for 10 minutes. Reheat the corn and zucchini filling in a skillet, and heat the puréed beans in a small saucepan. Arrange the sope shells on a serving platter. Spread a thin layer of puréed beans inside each shell. Spoon a teaspoon of the corn and zucchini filling on top. Add a small dollop of salsa. Scatter the optional romaine ribbons over the salsa and drizzle the optional crema Mexicana over the leaves. Finish with the crumbled cheese. Although the sopes are still good after they cool, serve them warm to start.

Cooking Notes

Parboiling Corn: Remove the husks and silk from the corn cob, trim the ends and cut the cob in half. Place the corn in a large saucepan, cover with water and bring to a boil over high heat. Reduce the heat to low and simmer until tender, about 4 minutes. Rinse the corn in cold water and set aside until cool enough to handle.

De-kernelling Corn: Stand the cut side of the cob on end. Move a knife down the cob, cutting the kernels away at their roots.

Little Black Bean & Corn Cakes

TORTITAS DE FRIJOLES NEGROS Y ELOTE

Mexicans have a deep appreciation for the many flavorful varieties of beans available in their markets. Long ago, in the valley of Mexico, hundreds of bean varieties were hybridized by master plant breeders for growth in varying climatic conditions, as well as for different flavors and sizes. Lima beans as big as your hand, bead-sized white beans and the "ayocote," a gorgeous eggplant-purple bean only found around Mexico City, are a few results of these early breeding programs. Many of these hybridized beans are now hitting the gourmet food scene in the US as "heirloom" beans. In this preparation, "frijoles negros," or black turtle beans, are made into corn-studded cakes. Serve them with a salad for a light meal, or as a side to Chile Chipotle Grilled Vegetables (page 98).

YIELDS 12 CAKES

For Advance Preparation and Assembly of the Dish

1 1/4 cup Oaxacan-Style Beans in Broth (page 115), or canned black beans, drained

1/3 cup crema Mexicana (page 20), drizzling consistency

1 recipe Fresh Tomato Salsa (page 42)

For the Bean Cakes

1/4 teaspoon coriander seeds

1/4 teaspoon cumin seeds

1 allspice berry

A 3/8-inch piece canela

1/8-1/4 teaspoon chile pequin

5 tablespoons safflower oil

1 ear corn, raw, kernels cut from the cob (see Cooking Notes, page 49)

1 chile serrano, stemmed, quartered lengthwise, seeds and membranes removed, minced

1/4 white onion, peeled and cut into 1/4-inch cubes

1 egg, lightly beaten

1/4 teaspoon salt, or to taste

4 tablespoons fresh cilantro (leaves only), coarsely chopped, 1/2 reserved for garnish

1 tablespoon all-purpose flour, for dusting

Toast the coriander, cumin, allspice, canela and chile pequin over medium-high heat until fragrant, about 2 minutes. Transfer to a spice/coffee grinder, pulverize into a powder and set aside. In a medium skillet, heat 1 tablespoon of the oil over medium-high heat. When hot, add the corn, chile and onion. Sauté until the onion softens and is translucent, about 4 minutes. Stir in the spice/chile powder. Remove the mixture from the heat. In a blender, coarsely purée the beans and egg together. Add the bean purée to the skillet and mix well. Add the salt and 2 tablespoons of the chopped cilantro. Stir to combine, taste for salt and set aside.

Preheat the oven to 200°F and dust a large plate with flour. Form a heaping tablespoon of the bean mixture into a cake about 2 inches in diameter and place it on the floured plate. The mixture will be very sticky, so reshape the cake on the plate if necessary. Continue in the same manner with the remaining bean mixture, making 12 cakes.

Line a baking pan with paper towels. In a large skillet, heat 2 tablespoons of the oil over medium-high heat. When hot, add 5-6 bean cakes and cook until brown and crisp, 2-3 minutes per side. Remove them from the skillet to the paper towel-lined baking pan and place in the oven to keep warm. Add 2 more tablespoons of oil to the skillet and cook the remaining bean cakes.

Place the bean cakes on individual plates, 2-3 cakes per person. Top with a drizzle of crema Mexicana and a sprinkling of the reserved cilantro. Add a couple of spoonfuls of salsa on the side and serve.

Tamale Dough

MASA PARA TAMALES

Originally left as treats at altars for ancient gods, tamales are still popular in Mexico, especially during festivals. The most typical wraps for these steamed masa treats are dried corn husks (see page 53). However, other wraps are frequently used—fresh corn husks, fresh corn leaves, banana leaves (see page 56) and even Swiss chard leaves (see page 59). Each wrapper adds its own flavor or quirk to the tamales. The variety of tamale fillings is endless. Try just about any of the fillings in this book (see Index, page 127), or experiment on your own!

YIELDS 8 TO 12 TAMALES, DEPENDING ON THE TYPE OF WRAPPER

2 tablespoons extra virgin olive oil

4 tablespoons vegetable shortening, such as Crisco

1 1/2 cups masa harina

1/2 teaspoon salt

1/2 teaspoon baking powder

1 cup broth, pork, light chicken (page 24) or vegetable (page 26), slightly warmed (refer to the tamale recipe you are using)

Beat the oil and shortening with an electric mixer until the volume increases and it is creamy, about 1 minute. Add the masa harina, salt and baking powder and beat until very small crumbs form. Add 3/4 cup of the broth in 3 parts, beating well after each addition. Test for texture—the dough should be moist, soft enough to easily plop out of a spoon and should not taste gritty. Add more broth, 1 tablespoon at a time, until the dough sticks slightly to the side of the bowl, but still comes out of a spoon easily. After achieving the correct texture, beat the dough at high speed for 5-10 minutes, frequently scraping the sides of the bowl. After 5 minutes, check to see if a small piece of dough will float in a cup of cold water. If it does not, keep beating. It takes a total of about 8 minutes to aerate the dough enough to ensure fluffy tamales. Set aside, but not too long before tamale preparation.

Tamales With Shredded Pork & Chile Guajillo

TAMALES CON CERDO Y CHILE GUAJILLO

Although tamales are eaten and adored by Mexicans on a regular basis, they are generally considered food for festivals, such as "Los Días de los Muertos," the Days of the Dead. This festival is a curiously merry remembrance of relatives and friends who have passed on. It is, of course, celebrated with plenty of good things to eat. By preparing the favorite dishes of the deceased, families hope to attract souls home on November 1 and 2. During this time, tamale making is often a party, "una tamalada," with guests participating in the assembly line as well as the consumption. For a casual supper with friends, serve with Beans in Broth (page 114) and Arroz a la Mexicana (page 112), and finish with Creamy Peppermint Gelatin with Mexican Chocolate Sauce (page 122).

SERVES 4 TO 5 ♦ YIELDS 10 TAMALES

For Tamale Assembly

2 ounces dried corn husks, about 4 ears' worth

1 recipe Tamale Dough (page 52), using pork broth reserved from the filling recipe

For the Pork and Guajillo Filling

2 tablespoons mixed oil (see page 15)

4 chiles guajillos, fried (see Techniques, page 17)

8 ounces boneless pork shoulder, cut into 1/2-inch cubes

3/4 teaspoon salt

1/4 white onion, peeled and coarsely chopped

3 plum tomatoes, seeded (see Techniques, page 19) and coarsely chopped

2 cloves garlic, peeled and coarsely chopped

1/8 teaspoon aniseed

1/8 teaspoon freshly ground black pepper

Preparing the Husks: Place the corn husks in a shallow bowl and cover with water at its boiling point. Weigh down with a plate and soak for 1 hour.

Preparing the Filling: Using the oil, prepare the chiles as instructed in Techniques and reserve the oil in the skillet. Soak the chiles for 45 minutes. Meanwhile, in a medium saucepan over high heat, combine the pork, 2 cups of cold water and 1/2 teaspoon of the salt and bring to a simmer. Reduce the heat to low and continue simmering until the pork is tender, about 30 minutes. Remove from the heat, skim the surface of any grey foam and let the pork cool in its broth. Drain 1 cup of the broth for the tamale dough and leave the rest with the pork. When cool enough to handle, shred the meat by pulling apart the pieces into strands with your fingers. Set aside.

Reheat the chile skillet and oil over medium-high heat. When hot, sauté the onion until it begins to brown, about 5 minutes. Add the tomatoes, stir to combine and cook until they soften, about 3 minutes. Transfer to a blender and add the drained chiles and the garlic. Purée the mixture and strain through a wire mesh sieve to remove the chile skin. Discard the skin and reserve 2 tablespoons of the sauce for the tamale dough. Stir the remaining sauce, the remaining 1/4 teaspoon salt, the aniseed and pepper into the shredded pork. Taste for balance of flavor, making adjustments for salt and pepper if necessary.

Preparing the Tamale Dough: Using the reserved pork broth, prepare the tamale dough according to the recipe. Blend the 2 tablespoons of reserved chile sauce into the dough with an electric mixer. The dough should now be a pale orange color. Set aside.

Assembling the Tamales: Drain the corn husks well. Separate them, reserving 10 of the largest for stuffing. From the remaining husks, split off 20 strands, 1/4 inch wide, to use as ties for the tamales, and save the rest to line the sides and bottom of the steamer. Prepare the steamer (see Cooking Notes below).

Place one of the 10 large husks on a work surface. Pat the inside dry and spread 2-3 tablespoons of the tamale dough in the center. To more easily spread the masa, hold down the long sides of the husk with your fingers on one side and thumb on the other. With the other hand, pat the masa into place and smooth into its final shape with your fingers—a rectangle approximately 2 1/2 x 3 1/2 inches and 3/8 inch thick, leaving about 1 1/2 inches of the husk free on all sides for securing the packet. If your husks are widely variant in size, adjust the amount of masa accordingly. Spoon a heaping tablespoon of filling down the center of the masa. To secure the tamale, bring the long sides of the husk together so that the edges meet. Fold down the joined edge 2-3 times until a snug seam is formed over the masa. Note: the masa is not supposed to overlap to enclose the filling. Leaving a little room for the masa to expand, twist the cut end of the husk and hold it down on the work surface with your thumb while securing with one of the husk ties. Do the same to secure the point end. Repeat for the other 9 large husks.

Decide how the tamales will best fit in the steamer basket, and place them all in the same manner to cook evenly. Transfer the filled basket to the simmering water. Cover tightly and steam the tamales until they easily separate from their wrappers, 50-60 minutes. Remove the wrapped tamales to a platter or individual plates and serve. A cautionary word: don't try to eat the husk, as did poor President Ford when attending a swanky Texan dinner. Unwrap the tamales from the inedible husks before eating.

Cooking Notes

Preparing a Tamale Steamer: It is best to use a steamer that has a flat bottom and fits over a large saucepan or Dutch oven that holds at least 1 quart of water. If you only have a vegetable basket steamer, make sure enough hot water is handy during the cooking time to add as the steamer water evaporates. When adding the water, lift the basket slightly to the side to avoid pouring the water over the tamale packets. If there is a handle in the middle of the steamer basket, a little foil may help to line it.

Use the remaining husks to line the sides and bottom of the steamer basket— this will prevent the steam from directly contacting the tamales. With the pointed sides of the husks pointing down, overlap the husks around the perimeter of the basket. Hold them in place with your hand if necessary until you cover the bottom. Once the bottom husks are in place, they will hold the husks on the sides in position. Your basket is now ready to be loaded with tamales.

As you prepare the tamales, bring 1 quart of water to a boil over high heat. When it reaches a boil, reduce the heat to low, keeping the water hot until the tamales are ready to be steamed.

Chicken Tamales Flavored With Fennel Greens

Try these tamales to sample many flavors uncommon in the American experience of Mexican food. They are truly delicious, and fun to make, especially if you pull some helpers into the kitchen. The banana leaves not only add exotic flair to the presentation, but impart a smoky flavor to the dish, not unlike artichoke leaves. This flavor, combined with hoja santa (see Cooking Notes below), is truly reminiscent of Oaxaca and other areas of southern Mexico. Frozen banana leaves can be found in many Mexican and Asian markets. Avoid brown leaves—they should definitely be green. If you cannot find banana leaves, you may make these tamales with corn husks by following the stuffing method on page 53.

Tamales freeze very well when stored in freezer bags. To reheat, remove them from the plastic and wrap securely in foil. Place the foil packets in a steamer basket for 30 minutes, or until heated through. Try these tamales as a starter course, followed by an entrée of Grilled Prawns in Achiote Citrus Marinade (page 90), a side of Swiss Chard Filling (page 104) and, for an elegant finish, a dessert of Spiced Crêpes with Goat Milk Caramel (page 118).

SERVES 4 ♦ YIELDS 8 TAMALES

For Advance Preparation and Tamale Assembly

1 recipe Cooked Green Salsa (page 44)

1 1/4 cups shredded chicken (page 25)

1/2 pound frozen banana leaves, thawed overnight and prepared (see Techniques, page 17), torn into 8 pieces about 8 inches square, plus 16 strips about 1/4 inch wide, and extra pieces for patching tears and for lining the steamer

1 recipe Tamale Dough (page 52), using light chicken broth

1/3 cup crema Mexicana (page 20), drizzling consistency

For the Shredded Chicken Filling in Tomatillo-Fennel Sauce
1 teaspoon safflower oil
Prepared Cooked Green Salsa
1 teaspoon dried epazote (leaves only)
1/2 teaspoon sugar
1/3 cup fresh fennel bulb, feathery parts only (see Cooking Notes below), chopped
3/4 teaspoon freshly ground black pepper
3/8 teaspoon salt, or to taste
Prepared shredded chicken

Preparing the Filling: Lightly coat a medium skillet with the oil and heat over medium-high heat. When hot, add the green salsa. Stir in the epazote, sugar, fennel, pepper and salt. Add the shredded chicken and stir to coat. Taste for balance of flavor, adding more salt if necessary. Set aside.

Assembling the Tamales: Prepare the tamale dough and banana leaves. Prepare the steamer (see Cooking Notes, page 55), using banana leaf remnants. Make sure the banana leaves have cooled before filling with masa, or the masa will melt. Arrange a leaf square on a flat work surface with the shiny side up. Spoon about 3 tablespoons of masa onto the farthest left edge of the leaf and spread evenly toward the center to form a 3/8-inch thick, 3 x 5-inch rectangle. The short side of the masa rectangle should be centered along the left edge of the leaf. Place 2 tablespoons of the chicken filling on the right half of the masa rectangle. Fold the leaf in thirds, with the left, masa-only side of the rectangle folding over the filling. Fold the final flap with no masa over the top. Overlap the ends over the seam. Secure the overlap with 1 or 2 leaf strips, making an attractive packet. Repeat with the remaining leaves.

Decide how the tamales will best fit in the steamer basket, and place them all in the same manner to cook evenly. Transfer the filled basket to the simmering water. Cover tightly and steam the tamales until they easily separate from their wrappers, 50-60 minutes. Remove the wrapped tamales to a platter or individual plates, and serve in their wrappers. To eat, unwrap the tamales from the inedible banana leaves and drizzle with a little crema Mexicana.

Cooking Notes

Achieving the Flavor of Hoja Santa: Hoja santa is a large leaf, bigger than your hand, used as a cooking herb in many southern Mexican dishes. The plant is related to the vine that produces black pepper. The flavor of hoja santa is distinctive, somewhat anise-like, but also peppery. It is hard to replicate, but the substitute suggested by Rick Bayless in his book, *Authentic Mexican,* does a good job by using a combination of fresh fennel and black pepper.

To prepare the fennel, select a fresh fennel bulb, also called anise, that has a lot of feathery greens on the stalks. Use only the feathery greenery, reserving the rest of the bulb for another use, such as Fennel and Leek Vegetable Broth (page 26). Roughly chop the greenery in the quantity specified for the recipe.

CRISP TOTOPOS AND QUESO IN EARTHENWARE
DISHES ARE READY TO BE SERVED AT EL BAJIO
RESTAURANT IN MEXICO CITY.

Tamales Wrapped in Swiss Chard Leaves

TAMALES DE ACELGAS

Chard makes a tasty edible wrapper for tamales, and is handy when banana leaves or corn husks are not available. Serve these corn and zucchini-filled tamales with Butternut Squash (page 100) as a side dish. Rustic Black Bean Soup (page 28), Chile Chipotle Grilled Vegetables (page 98) and Jicama, Pineapple and Watercress Salad (page 34) also make great accompaniments.

SERVES 6 ♦ YIELDS 12 TAMALES

1 pound Swiss chard, with very large leaves
1 recipe Corn and Zucchini Filling (page 47)
1 recipe Tamale Dough (page 52), using light chicken or vegetable broth
1/3 cup crema Mexicana (page 20), drizzling consistency

If the chard is sandy, immerse it in water and allow the sand to drop to the bottom of the sink or bowl. Rinse each leaf and trim off the stalk at the base of the greenery. Bring a large saucepan of water to a simmer over medium-high heat. Place the chard leaves in the pan and parboil until softened, about 1 1/2 minutes. Immediately drain the chard and immerse it in cold water. Drain again and separate 12 of the largest leaves from the pile. Use the rest of the leaves in preparing the tamale steamer (see Cooking Notes, page 55).

Lay a leaf flat, with the underside facing up, and pat dry. Place a heaping tablespoon of tamale dough near the base of the leaf. Flatten it into a 2 1/2- to 3-inch square, about 3/8 inch thick. Top with a spoonful of filling. If the sides of the leaf extend beyond the filling, bring them up against the filling. Wrap the remaining length of the leaf over the filling, securing the leaf tip on the underside. The weight of the packet will hold the tip in place. Using both hands, lay the packet flat in the steamer basket. Arrange the tamales in a single layer, cover tightly and steam until the masa is cooked through and easily separates from the leaves, about 45 minutes. Serve drizzled with crema Mexicana.

Enchiladas With Chile Sauce & Cabbage Relish

ENCHILADAS ROJAS

Enchiladas make their appearance in varying shapes throughout Mexico. Whether rolled, folded in half, folded in quarters or stacked like a layered tortilla cake, the only requirement to be an "enchilada" is to be chile-ed. This recipe combines the earthy flavors of chile-dipped corn tortillas and pinto beans with crispy marinated cabbage. It makes a perfect snack for Superbowl Sunday, around the third or fourth quarter. However, its colorful presentation also makes it beautiful enough for the first course of an elegant dinner party.

SERVES 4 TO 6 ♦ YIELDS 12 ENCHILADAS

For Advance Preparation and Enchilada Assembly

1 cup Refried Beans with Onion (page 116), preferably pinto bean version

1 recipe Pickled Green Cabbage Relish (page 38)

12 5 1/2-inch Corn Tortillas (page 106), or store-bought

3 tablespoons safflower oil

1/2-3/4 cup queso fresco, or mild feta cheese, crumbled

Garnish: Fresh cilantro sprigs

For the Chile Sauce—yields about 1 1/3 cups

4 tablespoons mixed oil (see page 15)

6 chiles guajillos, fried (see Techniques, page 17)

3 chiles anchos, fried (see Techniques, page 17)

6 large cloves garlic, roasted (see Techniques, page 19) and peeled

3/8 teaspoon cumin seeds, toasted

A 3/4-inch piece canela

3/8 teaspoon black peppercorns

1 1/2 cups light chicken or vegetable broth (page 24 or 26)

3/4 teaspoon salt

2-5 teaspoons sugar, to taste

Preparing the Sauce: Using the oil, prepare the chiles as instructed in Techniques. Soak the chiles for 45 minutes. Coarsely mash the garlic with a fork and transfer to a blender. In a spice/coffee grinder, pulverize the cumin, canela and peppercorns. Add the spices to the blender along with the broth and salt. Drain the chiles, reserving 1/4 cup of the soaking liquid, and add both to the blender. Purée the mixture, strain through a sieve and discard the chile skin. Taste the chile sauce for bitterness. If bitter, add the sugar, 1 teaspoon at a time, until the flavor is pleasant, but not sweet. Adjust for salt if necessary.

Assembling the Enchiladas: Preheat the oven to 200°F. Line a baking pan with foil and place it in the oven. Tear off 6 sheets of foil measuring 4 x 12 inches and set aside. Transfer the chile sauce to a small skillet, at least as big as the tortillas, and warm over medium heat. When the mixture begins to bubble, stir and reduce the heat to warm. Heat the beans, stirring in a little water if they seem dry. In a medium skillet, heat the oil over medium-high heat. Line a plate with paper towels and place to the side of the large skillet. Set a small plate for assembling the enchiladas near the chile sauce, beans and cheese.

When the oil is very hot, lay a tortilla flat in the oil and cook until soft, about 4 seconds. Using tongs, transfer the tortilla to the paper towel-lined plate and blot any excess oil. Using your fingers, lay the softened tortilla in the chile sauce. Press the tortilla down to coat, turn it over and coat the other side. Do not linger too long, or the tortilla will become soggy and break apart. Transfer the tortilla to the small plate. Place a heaping tablespoon of the beans in the center and sprinkle with a little cheese. Fold the tortilla in half and then in half again to form lazy quarters—the corners will not quite meet. With a spatula, transfer the enchilada to the baking pan and cover with a piece of foil, leaving space for another enchilada on the same layer. Continue in the same manner, layering a piece of foil over each pair of enchiladas.

To serve, spoon 3/4 cup of the cabbage relish onto each plate. Use the foil to lift each pair of enchiladas out of the pan, and slide them on top or to the side of the cabbage. Spread a teaspoon of the remaining chile sauce over each enchilada, sprinkle with crumbled cheese, garnish with cilantro and serve.

Shredded Crab Tacos With Pickled Red Onions

TACOS DE JAIBA

Mexicans generally regard their tortilla-in-the-dish specialties—quesadillas, tacos and enchiladas—as snacks. These delectable tortilla preparations are never served for "la comida," the day's main meal, taken at 2 PM. Instead, they are eaten out on the town, or hastily at home while standing over the hot "comal," or griddle, as the fresh tortillas are removed. However, we Americanos may eat these snacks with complete abandon at the dinner table, without a scolding "abuelita," or grandmother, pointing a finger at our hasty meal. By the way, Mexican tacos are never found crisp-fried as they are in the United States.

Delicious taco fillings abound in Mexico and are a part of an unrecognized class of culinary expertise. Serve these soft crab tacos on a platter, topped with a scattering of pickled red onions. Roasted corn and Fresh Tomato Salsa (page 42) make satisfying accompaniments. For a light supper, serve after a first course of Chicken Soup with Lime and Tortilla Strips (page 30).

SERVES 4 TO 6 ♦ YIELDS 12 TACOS

For Taco Assembly

1/2 recipe Pickled Red Onions (page 35)

12 5 1/2-inch Corn Tortillas (page 106), or store-bought

For the Crab and Cabbage Filling

3 tablespoons safflower oil

1/2 white onion, peeled and minced

3 cloves garlic, peeled and minced

1/2 teaspoon coriander seeds, toasted and ground

5 allspice berries, toasted and ground

1 teaspoon dried epazote (leaves only)

2 small plum tomatoes, seeded (see Techniques, page 19) and finely chopped

1/3 green cabbage, shredded (see Cooking Notes, page 38), about 3 cups

3 tablespoons fresh cilantro, coarsely chopped
1/2 teaspoon freshly ground black pepper
1/4 teaspoon salt, to taste
3 quarters of a lime
1/2 pound lump crab meat
2 tablespoons bitter orange juice (page 20)

Preparing the Filling: Heat the oil in a large skillet over medium-high heat. When hot, add the onion and garlic. Sauté until the onion is soft, but not brown, about 5 minutes. Stir in the coriander, allspice and epazote. Add the tomatoes and continue to sauté until the tomatoes lose their rawness and the color deepens, 2-3 minutes. Add the cabbage, stir to combine, and cook until soft, 5-7 minutes. Add a little water if the mixture starts to stick to the skillet. Stir in the cilantro, pepper and salt. Squeeze the lime over the top and stir once or twice more. Remove the skillet from the heat.

In a medium bowl, break the crab into even bite-sized pieces and toss with the bitter orange juice. Set aside.

Assembling the Tacos: Heat a large skillet over medium-high heat. When very hot, spread 3 tortillas on the bottom of the dry skillet—they will overlap a little. Heat the tortillas for 30 seconds, flip and continue heating until air pockets form and they are soft, about 45 seconds. Remove the tortillas from the heat one at a time, and place 2 tablespoons of the cabbage mixture in the center of the tortilla, topping it with 2 tablespoons of the crab. Fold the tortilla in half and place on a platter. Make each taco quickly in a similar manner and arrange on the platter so they overlap. Top with the pickled onions and serve.

Soft Tacos With Yucatán-Style Shredded Pork

TACOS SUAVES DE COCHINITA PIBIL

In this classic dish from the Yucatán, banana leaves lend an earthy, smoky flavor to the savory achiote-marinated pork. In a pinch, foil may be substituted for the banana leaves. Slow baking makes the pork deliciously tender and easy to tear into tasty morsels with a fork or fingers. Serve the tortillas and pickled red onions on the side, allowing each person to make their own tacos as hunger demands. Accompany with a simple salad of sliced avocado and marinated beefsteak tomatoes. Cold Mexican beer makes a great complement to the flavor of these tacos. When making this dish, plan ahead—the pork requires overnight or all-day marination, plus 2 1/2 hours baking time.

SERVES 4 TO 6

For Advance Preparation and Taco Assembly

1 recipe Yucatecan Achiote Paste (page 21)

2 recipes bitter orange juice (page 20)

1/4 pound frozen banana leaves, thawed overnight and prepared (see Techniques, page 17), torn into 2 pieces about 8 x 12 inches, plus extra pieces for patching tears

1 recipe Pickled Red Onions (page 35)

12 5 1/2-inch Corn Tortillas (page 106), or store-bought

For the Achiote Marinade

6 cloves garlic, roasted (see Techniques, page 19) and peeled

3 tablespoons prepared Yucatecan Achiote Paste

5 tablespoons prepared bitter orange juice

2 teaspoons dried Mexican oregano

1 teaspoon freshly ground black pepper

1/4 teaspoon salt

2 pounds pork tenderloin

Preparing the Marinade: In a small bowl, mash the garlic with a fork and mix in the remaining marinade ingredients. Place the pork in a non-metallic baking dish. Rub the marinade into the meat, cover and refrigerate for at least 6 hours.

For the Pibil Parcel

2 tablespoons prepared bitter orange juice

2 tablespoons extra virgin olive oil

3 chiles güeros (or Anaheim or Hungarian wax), roasted and cut into rajas (see Techniques, page 18)

1/2 red onion, peeled and sliced into thin half moons

1/4 teaspoon dried marjoram

1/4 teaspoon dried thyme

8 bay leaves

1 teaspoon safflower oil

Preparing the Pibil Parcel: Preheat the oven to 350°F, with the rack in the middle position. Remove the pork from the marinade to a plate. Whisk the bitter orange juice and olive oil into the marinade and set aside. Lay a large piece of foil on a work surface. Place one of the leaf pieces horizontally on the foil, with the shiny side of the leaf facing upwards. Cover any tears in the leaf with more wide strips. In the center of the leaf, place half of the chile strips and onions, and sprinkle with 1/8 teaspoon each of marjoram and thyme. Top with 4 bay leaves and place the pork on top of the herbs. Pour the marinade over the meat and cover with the remaining chile strips, onions, marjoram, thyme and bay leaves. Place the second leaf piece on top, with the shiny side facing the pork, and wrap the leaves to form a parcel. Wrap the foil around the parcel. Place in a roasting pan and roast for 2 1/2 hours. Remove from the oven and let stand 15-20 minutes. Unwrap the parcel and remove the pork to a bowl. Discard the bay leaves, transfer the remaining juices, chiles and onions to a large skillet and set aside. Arrange the banana leaves in a casserole dish just large enough to fit the pork and set aside. Shred the pork into bite-sized pieces and add to the skillet with the chiles and onions. Heat through and transfer to the leaf-lined dish.

Assembling the Tacos: Reheat the tortillas (see Cooking Notes, page 107) and serve with the heated pork filling and pickled onions, allowing each person to assemble their own tacos.

Tostadas With Potatoes & Garlic

TOSTADAS CON PAPAS Y AJO

Potatoes, garlic and chiles are a delicious combination, and they are taken to new gastronomic heights when layered on a tostada with marinated cabbage, a drizzle of guacamole and a crumbling of queso fresco. Your taste buds will be tingling with delight at each bite. Serve these as part of a festive buffet including Eggs with Rajas and Epazote (page 92), Pueblan Five Vegetable Green Mole (page 96), Tamales with Shredded Pork and Chile Guajillo (page 53) and Arroz Blanco (page 110). Note: If you are preparing food for a party, the potato and garlic filling may be made a day ahead and reheated before using.

SERVES 6 ♦ YIELDS 12 TOSTADAS

For Advance Preparation and Tostada Assembly

2/3 recipe (3 cups) Pickled Green Cabbage Relish (page 38)

1/3 recipe (1 cup) Guacamole (page 39), puréed in a blender with 3 tablespoons water, 1 teaspoon lime juice and a pinch of salt

12 5 1/2-inch Corn Tortillas (page 106), or store-bought

4 tablespoons peanut or safflower oil, for preparing the tostada shells

1/2 cup queso fresco, or mild feta cheese, crumbled

For the Potato and Garlic Filling

4 tablespoons mixed oil (see page 15)

3 chiles guajillo, fried (see Techniques, page 17)

2 chiles pasillas, fried (see Techniques, page 17)

6 cloves garlic, roasted (see Techniques, page 19) and peeled

4 teaspoons cider vinegar

1/2 teaspoon salt, or to taste

1 teaspoon sugar

1/2 white onion, peeled and cut into 1/4-inch cubes

1 pound red boiling potatoes (about 5 medium), cut into 1/4-inch cubes

1/2 cup orange juice

4 teaspoons epazote

Preparing the Filling: Using the oil, prepare the chiles as instructed in Techniques and reserve the oil in the skillet. Soak the chiles for 45 minutes. Drain the chiles and transfer them to a blender along with 1/3 cup of the soaking liquid. Add the garlic, vinegar, salt and sugar to the blender and purée into a very smooth sauce. Taste for balance of flavor, adding more vinegar, salt or sugar if needed.

Reheat the chile skillet and oil over medium heat. When hot, add the onion and sauté until translucent, about 4 minutes. Add the potatoes and sauté for 5 minutes, stirring occasionally. Mix in the chile purée and cook until the mixture becomes dry, stirring frequently, about 6 minutes. Stir in 2 cups of cold water, the orange juice and epazote. Mix well, reduce the heat to low, cover and simmer until the potatoes are tender, 25-30 minutes. The sauce will dry out near the end of the cooking time. Keep the mixture warm.

Preparing the Tostada Shells: In a medium skillet, heat the oil over medium-high heat. When hot, add a tortilla and fry until golden and crisp, about 1 minute per side. Place on a paper towel-lined baking sheet and blot the excess oil. Continue until all the tortillas are fried. If not using immediately, place in a 150°F oven to keep warm until ready to serve.

(For lower-fat tostadas, brush the tortillas with olive oil, place them on a baking sheet and broil 3 inches from the heat for about 2 1/2 minutes. Turn once and cook until crisp, about 2 1/2 more minutes. Keep warm in a 150°F oven until ready to serve.)

Assembling the Tostadas: Spread each tostada shell with 2-3 tablespoons filling and top with 1-2 tablespoons cabbage relish. Drizzle 1-2 teaspoons guacamole over the cabbage and sprinkle with 1 teaspoon cheese. Serve warm.

Quesadillas With Chicken & Corn Mushrooms

This recipe was developed under the assumption that you will not be able to find cuitlacoche anywhere. An unusual Mexican delicacy, cuitlacoche, a sort of mushroom-like growth on corn, can be experienced at its best in and around Mexico City during the August rainy season. During this time, the ladies who make fresh hot masa snacks in the markets top them with sautéed cuitlacoche and squash blossoms. The flavors are quite simply of another world. The taste is so wonderful, as well as characteristic of central Mexico's rainy season, that it seemed impossible to omit it from this book. The taste of the shitake mushroom—aromatic, smoky and cheeselike—comes quite close to that of cuitlacoche when combined with puréed corn. Serve accompanied by Black Bean and Corn Salsa (page 40) and a fruit salad. As alternatives to the filling in this recipe, try making the quesadillas with Swiss Chard Filling (page 104) or Sweet Potato and Black Bean Picadillo (page 102), replacing the Epazote-Tomato sauce with salsa (see pages 41-44).

SERVES 6 ♦ YIELDS 14 QUESADILLAS

For Quesadilla Assembly

14 *5 1/2-inch Corn Tortillas (page 106), or store-bought*

1-2 tablespoons mixed oil (see page 15), for softening tortillas

1/2 cup queso fresco, or mild feta cheese, crumbled

Garnish: Fresh cilantro sprigs

For the Epazote-Tomato Sauce

9 plum tomatoes, peeled, seeded (see Techniques, page 19) and roughly chopped

3 chiles serranos (about 2 inches each), stemmed, quartered lengthwise, seeds and membranes removed

6 cloves garlic, peeled and chopped

1 1/2 teaspoons rice vinegar

1 1/2 teaspoons dried epazote (leaves only)
3/4 cup light chicken or vegetable broth (page 24 or 26)
3/4 teaspoon salt
1 tablespoon mixed oil (see page 15)

Preparing the Sauce: Purée the tomatoes, chiles, garlic, vinegar, epazote, broth and salt in a blender until smooth. In a large skillet, heat the oil over medium-high heat. When very hot, add the purée and sauté, stirring occasionally, until the mixture loses its rawness and the color deepens, about 5 minutes. Set aside.

For the Chicken and Cuitlacoche Filling

4 medium fresh shitake mushrooms (about 2 ounces), or 4 large reconstituted (soaking liquid reserved)

6 large button mushrooms (about 4 ounces)

1 tablespoon mixed oil (see page 15)

4 cloves garlic, peeled and minced

1 cup light chicken or vegetable broth (page 24 or 26)

2 teaspoons dried epazote (leaves only)

2 tablespoons rice vinegar

1 teaspoon black peppercorns, cracked (pulse twice in a spice/coffee grinder)

1 cup shredded chicken (page 25), or cubed cooked potato (vegetarian option)

2 tablespoons corn kernels, fresh, canned or frozen

Preparing the Filling: To clean the fresh mushrooms, wipe them with a damp paper towel—do not immerse them in water or they will absorb it. Trim the stems and cut the mushrooms into 1/4-inch slices. Set aside. In a medium skillet, heat the oil over medium-high heat. When hot, add the garlic and sauté until it begins to brown, 2-3 minutes. Add the mushrooms, plus the soaking liquid if reconstituted, the broth, epazote, vinegar and pepper. Stir to mix, reduce the heat to low and simmer until the mushrooms are well cooked and a little juice remains, about 5 minutes. Stir in the chicken or potato. Purée the corn in a blender with 2 tablespoons of water, and add to the mushroom mixture with 1/2 cup of the Epazote-Tomato Sauce. Return the mixture to a simmer over medium-high heat and reduce the liquid just until it holds between the solids when stirred, about 5 minutes. Set aside.

Softening the Tortillas: Lay out the tortillas to dry for a few minutes—there should be no excess moisture. Line a plate with paper towels. Add enough oil to a large skillet to coat the bottom, about 1 tablespoon. Heat the skillet over medium-high heat. When very hot, add 2 tortillas and cook until they are soft, about 4 seconds. Transfer the tortillas to the paper towel-lined plate. Stack them with a paper towel between each one to blot excess oil. In the same manner, adding more oil to the skillet if necessary, continue the softening and blotting process until all of the tortillas are in a stack. Reserve the skillet.

Preparing the Quesadillas: Preheat the oven to 200°F. Line a baking pan with foil and place it in the oven. To prepare the quesadillas, place a heaping tablespoon of filling in the center of a tortilla in a cigar shape and top with a teaspoon of cheese. Fold the tortilla in half and set aside. Continue in the same manner with the remaining tortillas. After the tortillas are stuffed, wipe any excess oil from the large skillet and place over medium-high heat. When hot, add as many quesadillas as will fit in a single layer. Cook the quesadillas, gently flattening them with the back of a spatula, until they are golden, about 4 minutes per side. As the quesadillas finish cooking, place them in the oven and keep them covered with foil. Just before cooking the last of the quesadillas, reheat the remaining Epazote-Tomato Sauce.

Assembling the Dish: Place the quesadillas, 2 each, on plates and spoon 2 tablespoons of the warm Epazote-Tomato Sauce over each quesadilla. Top with a little crumbled cheese and a sprig of cilantro. Serve immediately.

ONE OF ABOUT 75 LIKE IT IN THE TINY TOWN OF CHOLULA,
THIS CHURCH WAS BUILT BY THE SPANISH
OVER THE RUINS OF A PRE-COLUMBIAN CHOLULTEC TEMPLE.
EVEN CHOLULA'S GREAT PYRAMID, THE LARGEST
IN THE WORLD, NOW HAS A CHRISTIAN CHURCH RESTING
ON ITS CROWN.

Pork, Beef, Poultry, Fish & Egg Entrées

Roast Pork Loin in Adobo

CERDO EN ADOBO

This is the perfect meat dish for a barbecue. Just pack the pork in its marinade and grill when the coals are hot. Serve with the colorful Jicama, Pineapple and Watercress Salad (page 34), or try it with Chayotes Stuffed with Tomatoes and Herbs (page 94) as a warm salad. Leftover slices of pork may be tucked into warm tortillas for a light lunch. For a tender, flavorful piece of meat, marinate the pork tenderloin in the adobo for as long as possible.

SERVES 4 TO 6

1 recipe Chile Adobo Marinade (page 22)

1 cup orange juice

1 teaspoon sugar

2 pounds pork tenderloin

Garnish: Orange slices and fresh cilantro sprigs

In a medium bowl, combine the adobo marinade, orange juice and sugar, and mix well. Place the tenderloin in a non-metallic baking dish or bowl, cover with half of the adobo-orange sauce, reserving the other half. Turn the pork to coat all sides, cover and refrigerate for 8 hours or overnight. Occasionally turn the tenderloin in the marinade. Remove the meat from the refrigerator an hour before roasting so that it is not cold when placed in the oven.

Preheat the oven to 475°F. Cover the baking dish with foil and roast the meat, occasionally basting with its juices. After 20 minutes, turn over the tenderloin, baste and roast for 20 more minutes, or until a meat thermometer inserted deeply into the roast reads 160°F. Remove from the oven and let stand covered for 10-15 minutes. Heat the reserved adobo-orange sauce in a saucepan over medium-high heat until hot. Slice the pork and arrange on a platter. Spoon the heated sauce over the pork and garnish with orange slices and sprigs of cilantro.

Chiles Rellenos With Savory Pork Picadillo

In the cuisines of many cultures, the combination of sweet and savory is intriguing and utterly delicious, but few preparations can match the Oaxacan picadillo. This version combines shredded pork with raisins, toasted almonds and canela to make a filling for battered and fried ancho chiles. The ancho, a dried chile, is an unusual twist on the roasted chile poblano relleno with which we are familiar, and its sweet heat is a perfect match for the picadillo filling. This dish is well complemented by the Arroz Blanco (page 110) topped with fried plantains. It also makes an excellent filling for quesadillas (page 68). The filling may be prepared a day in advance and refrigerated.

YIELDS 6 CHILES RELLENOS

For Chile Relleno Assembly

1 recipe Epazote-Tomato Sauce (page 68)

Garnish: 1/4 cup fresh cilantro (leaves only), chopped

For the Picadillo Filling

2 tablespoons mixed oil (see page 15)

3/4 pound boneless pork loin, cut into 1-inch cubes

1 small white onion, peeled, 1/2 cut into 2 wedges and 1/2 coarsely chopped

4 cloves garlic, peeled and crushed with a mallet or the side of a knife

1 bay leaf

1 chile chipotle, stem, seeds and membranes removed

1/4 cup orange juice

1/3 cup raisins

2 plum tomatoes, seeded (see Techniques, page 19) and quartered

3 whole cloves

A 1-inch piece canela

1/4 teaspoon black peppercorns

1/4 cup blanched slivered almonds, toasted and coarsely chopped

1/2 tablespoon cider vinegar

1/4 teaspoon freshly ground black pepper

3/8 teaspoon salt

Preparing the Picadillo: In a small saucepan, heat 1 tablespoon of the oil over medium-high heat. When hot, add the pork and sauté for 3-5 minutes. Add the 2 onion wedges, half of the garlic, the bay leaf, chile chipotle and enough water to barely cover the meat. Bring the mixture to a simmer, reduce the heat to very low, cover and continue to simmer until the pork is tender, 30-35 minutes.

While the pork is cooking, combine the raisins and orange juice to cover in a small bowl and set aside. Transfer the chopped onion, remaining garlic and tomatoes to a blender and set aside. In a spice/coffee grinder, pulverize the cloves, canela and peppercorns into a powder. Add the spice powder to the blender.

Remove the cooked pork from the heat. Add 1/2 cup of the broth and the chile chipotle to the blender. Discard the onion, garlic and bay leaf, and set the saucepan aside, allowing the meat to cool in its broth. When cool enough to handle, shred the pork by pulling apart the pieces into strands with your fingers. Set aside.

Purée the tomato/chipotle mixture into a smooth sauce. In a large skillet, heat the remaining tablespoon of oil over medium-high heat. When hot, add the tomato/chipotle sauce and cook, stirring occasionally, until the sauce has thickened, about 5 minutes. Add the shredded pork, raisins, orange juice and almonds, and cook until the mixture is dry. Season with the vinegar, pepper and salt. Stir to combine and taste for balance of flavor. Set aside to cool.

For the Chiles Anchos

6 large chiles anchos (whole and untorn), rinsed and dried

2 tablespoons safflower oil

Flour for dusting

3 eggs, separated

3/4 cup oil, preferably peanut or safflower, for frying
A pinch of salt

Preparing the Chiles: To open each chile, use a sharp paring knife to make a vertical slit near the stem. Use the same knife, or kitchen shears, to cut along one side to the tip, being careful not to tear the chile. Carefully open the chile and remove the seeds and membranes. Repeat for each chile.

In a medium skillet, heat the 2 tablespoons of safflower oil over medium-high heat. Line a plate with paper towels. When the oil is very hot, fry the chiles one at a time, using tongs to hold each side in the oil for 3-4 seconds. The chiles will expand a little. Be careful not to burn the skins or they will be bitter. Drain the chiles on the paper towel-lined plate. Place the chiles in a large bowl and cover with water at its boiling point. Weigh them down with a plate and let soak for no longer than 5 minutes to soften. Drain the chiles well and pat dry.

Stuffing and Frying the Chiles: Stuff each chile generously with the picadillo filling, allowing room to close the slit. Set the stuffed chiles aside. Sprinkle the flour on a large plate. Holding the slit closed, roll each of the stuffed chiles in the flour to lightly coat. Use your fingers to dust missed spots and remove excess flour from other areas. Set aside.

Preheat the oven to 250°F. Line a baking pan with paper towels and place in the oven. Beat the egg whites and a pinch of salt with an electric mixer until they form stiff peaks. In a separate bowl, use a fork to beat the egg yolks lightly, one at a time, and fold into the egg whites to completely combine. Fill a large skillet with the 3/4 cup oil, 1/2 inch deep, and heat over medium-high heat.

Using tongs or your fingers, quickly dip a chile into the egg batter to lightly coat. Spoon batter over any missed spots. Place the most smoothly battered side of the chile in the oil and fry until golden brown, about 60 seconds. As the first side cooks, repair any holes in the batter on the top side by spooning more batter to cover. Gently turn over the chile with tongs and cook for 60 seconds longer. Transfer the chile to the pan in the oven to drain and keep warm. Repeat with the remaining chiles.

Assembling the Dish: Reheat the Epazote-Tomato Sauce. Serve the chiles topped with the heated sauce and a sprinkling of cilantro.

Roasted Beef Tenderloin

CARNE ASADA

This preparation of beef tenderloin, cooked until succulent and bursting with flavor, showcases a good piece of meat through simple seasoning. "Carne asada" translates as flame-cooked meat, so light a charcoal grill and sear the marinated tenderloin. Alternatively, a broiler may be used. For a menu suited to Indian summer, serve the grilled meat with the Roasted Tomatillo Salsa, warm Flour Tortillas (page 108) and Chile Chipotle Grilled Vegetables (page 98). To ward off the chill of winter, accompany the meat with Swiss Chard (page 104) and Butternut Squash (page 100). Leftovers make a terrific filling for soft tacos, topped with a spoonful of Chipotle Salsa (page 41).

SERVES 4

3/4 teaspoon coriander seeds, toasted

3/4 teaspoon cumin seeds, toasted

3/4 teaspoon black peppercorns

2 pounds beef tenderloin, trimmed of excess fat and cut into 4 pieces about 2 inches thick

1 1/2 limes, quartered

1 recipe Roasted Tomatillo Salsa (page 43)

In a spice/coffee grinder, pulverize the coriander, cumin and peppercorns into a coarse powder. Place the meat in a single layer in a non-metallic baking dish and squeeze half of the lime quarters over the steaks. Sprinkle with half of the ground spice mixture. Turn over the meat and repeat with the remaining lime and spices. Cover and let marinate in the refrigerator for 1 hour.

Prepare a charcoal grill. When the coals are ready (you'll be able to hold your hand at grill level for only 3-4 seconds), brush the grill rack with oil and place it over the coals. Cook the tenderloin, turning once, until the meat reaches the desired degree of doneness. If broiling, place the pan 3 inches from the heat and cook for 7-10 minutes on each side. Serve topped with salsa.

Roasted Turkey With Mole Poblano

MOLE POBLANO DE GUAJOLOTE

From the Seven Moles of Oaxaca to this classic dish from Puebla, mole is a food of celebration. It comes in a kaleidoscopic array of colors, from the black "El Rey," meaning The King, to green, red, yellow and brown. Dried red chiles, green chiles, vegetables, meats, seeds, nuts, spices and chocolate all have their places in various mole recipes.

Whatever the mole, the secret to a delicious one is mindful preparation. Chiles, vegetables, seeds and spices are carefully prepared by frying, roasting or toasting. These processes deepen and release the flavor from each ingredient. Near the end of preparation, the mole paste undergoes dry frying, a technique used by Mexican cooks to meld and concentrate flavor.

Preparing this recipe is essentially a 3-hour crash course in the many culinary techniques unique to Mexican cooking, with absolutely delicious results. The recipe calls for ingredients in groups, with their applicable methodology immediately following the list. Also, all of the techniques are described within the body of the recipe, rather than referencing the Techniques section, which should aid you in your crash course.

Both the sauce and the turkey may be prepared 1-2 days in advance and reheated to serve. Arroz Blanco (page 110) and Corn Tortillas (page 106) are the perfect accompaniments, and Veracruz-Style Red Snapper with Olives and Chiles (page 84) makes a sumptuous first course. For a vegetarian mole, use vegetable broth in the sauce, and firm tofu or tempeh instead of turkey. As a rather unorthodox alternative for serving the sauce, try it over simply prepared jumbo prawns—it's delicious. Mole leftovers make fabulous enchiladas, too.

SERVES 8 TO 10 ♦ YIELDS 6 CUPS SAUCE

1 tablespoon mixed oil (see page 15)
1/2 large turkey breast, with skin and bones (about 4-5 pounds)

77

Roasting the Turkey: Preheat the oven to 350°F. In a Dutch oven, heat the oil over medium-high heat and brown the turkey on all sides, about 3 minutes per side. Cover the pan with foil and roast until the juices run clear, or until a meat thermometer inserted deeply into the roast reads 180°F, 1-1 1/2 hours. Remove the turkey from the pan and let stand 10 minutes before slicing. Remove the skin and carve the turkey from the bone. Set aside until assembling the dish.

3 small or 2 large chiles mulatos
3 small or 2 large chiles anchos
2 chiles pasillas
1 chile chipotle
1/2 cup mixed oil (see page 15)

Frying the Chiles: Wipe each chile with a moist towel to remove dust. Cut along the sides of each chile with a knife or scissors, creating flat halves. Remove the stems, seeds and membranes, reserving 1 1/2 teaspoons of the seeds for toasting and grinding. Line a baking sheet with paper towels. In a medium skillet, heat the oil over medium heat. When hot, use tongs to press a chile piece in the oil. Fry for 4 seconds on each side. The inside will turn a warm tobacco color. Be careful not to burn the chiles, or the mole will be bitter. Fry each chile piece in the same manner, and drain on the paper towel-lined baking sheet. Reserve the chile-infused oil in the skillet for later use. Transfer the chiles to a large bowl and cover with water at its boiling point. Weigh down the chiles with a plate and soak for at least 30 minutes, but not more than 2 hours.

10 ounces tomatillos (about 7 small to medium), husks removed and washed
1 plum tomato
1/2 small white onion, unpeeled and halved
3 large cloves garlic, unpeeled

Roasting the Vegetables: Preheat the broiler to 500°F. Line a roasting pan with foil and place the tomatillos, tomato and onion, peel facing upward, in the pan. Roast until cooked through, about 10 minutes for small tomatillos and 20 minutes for larger tomatillos, tomato and onion. Turn the larger vegetables after 10 minutes to ensure even roasting. Meanwhile, heat a dry skillet over medium-high heat and roast the garlic, turning occasionally, until soft, 10-15 minutes.

Set aside. Transfer the tomatillos and any roasting liquid to a large bowl. Peel the tomato and add it to the bowl. Peel the onion, chop finely, mash with the back of a fork into a coarse pulp and add it to the bowl. Peel the garlic, mash with the fork and add it to the bowl. Use the fork to mash the mixture together. Remove the tomatillo skins, chop finely and add them back to the bowl. Continue mashing until the paste is well-mixed.

1/4 teaspoon coriander seeds
1/8 teaspoon aniseed
1/4 cup sesame seeds, plus 1 tablespoon for garnish
2 whole cloves
A 1/2-inch piece canela
1/4 teaspoon black peppercorns

Toasting and Grinding the Spices and Seeds: In a medium skillet, toast the coriander, aniseed and reserved chile seeds over medium-high heat until they release their aroma, 2-3 minutes. Transfer to a spice/coffee grinder. Toast the 1/4 cup of sesame seeds until light brown, about 4 minutes, and add to the grinder. Add the cloves, canela and peppercorns to the grinder and pulverize into a fine powder, rocking the grinder upside down repeatedly. Add the powder to the tomato bowl and use the fork to mash the spices into the mixture.

1/4 cup blanched slivered almonds
1/4 cup pepitas (green pumpkin seeds), unsalted
1/4 cup peanuts, unskinned and unsalted
3 tablespoons raisins
1 corn tortilla, laid out to dry and broken into large pieces
1/2 large croissant, or 1 thick slice bread (about 1 3/4 ounces), laid out to dry

Frying the Nuts and Breads: Reheat the chile skillet and oil over medium heat. Fry the ingredients separately, transferring them with a slotted spoon to a paper towel-lined baking sheet. Fry the almonds until golden brown, about 3 minutes. Keeping a lid handy for popping seeds, fry the pepitas until they pop, about 30 seconds, being careful not to let them brown. Fry the peanuts until light golden brown, 3-4 minutes. Fry the raisins until they swell. Fry the tortilla pieces until crisp. Break the bread into pieces and fry until golden and crisp.

Pulverizing the Ingredients: Mix the fried almonds, pepitas, peanuts and raisins together and transfer in batches to a spice/coffee grinder. Pulverize each batch into a powder, rocking the grinder upside down repeatedly. Transfer each batch to the tomato bowl and work it into the paste with the fork. This process achieves the dry maceration and blending of flavors that a blender or food processor cannot accomplish. Add the fried tortilla and bread and break them apart with the fork. Continue to mash until the paste is the consistency of muffin or quick bread batter. Transfer to a blender. Purée, scraping along the top and pushing down along the side with a wooden spoon to force the mixture past the blades. Do not let the blades hit the spoon. Purée until the paste is very fine and dry, about 3 minutes if you started with a fairly fine paste. Only if you absolutely must, add 1 tablespoon of water at a time to free the blades.

2 tablespoons mixed oil (see page 15)
1 1/2 ounces Mexican-style chocolate, finely chopped or in powdered form
4 cups light chicken or vegetable broth (page 24 or 26)

Dry Frying the Paste: Remove the paste to a bowl and clean the blender. Drain the chiles, reserving 1/2 cup of the soaking liquid, and add the chiles and liquid to the blender. Purée until smooth. In a large saucepan, heat the oil over medium heat. Add the chile purée and sauté, stirring constantly, until it becomes very dark and requires scraping from the sides and bottom of the pan in order to stir, 5-10 minutes. Add the tomato paste and stir until the mixture darkens and begins to clump, about 5 minutes. Add the chocolate, stir and fry for 8 minutes. The paste will clump and give off its oil during this time. Add the broth, stir to mix and cover. Reduce the heat to low and simmer for 40 minutes, stirring occasionally and making sure the mixture does not dry out. When the mole is finished cooking, dark oil will appear on the surface and the sauce will be thick enough to coat a spoon. Taste for salt, making adjustments if necessary.

Assembling the Dish: Preheat the oven to 350°F. Spoon some sauce into the bottom of an attractive baking dish. Arrange the turkey slices in the dish, pour the remaining sauce on top and cover with foil. Heat until warmed through, 20-25 minutes. Sprinkle with the remaining sesame seeds and serve.

Chicken in Green Pumpkin Seed Sauce

POLLO EN PEPIÁN VERDE

In the food halls of the town markets, and in Mexican homes, "cazuelas," or earthenware pots, are used to simmer many delectable sauces, such as moles and pepiáns. Pepián sauces are ancient, even pre-dating the Aztecs. They can be red or green, but they are always thickened with seeds and nuts, creating an earthy texture and flavor. Red pepián is colored by chiles, and it is prepared throughout Mexico. Green pepián is commonly found in Puebla, and variations are called mole verde in other parts of Mexico. Pepián is a classic of Mexican cooking and its preparation will surely summon your thoughts back to another time and culture, as you toast and grind the seeds for your sauce. Arroz Blanco (page 110) and fresh tortillas (page 106 or 108) are the perfect accompaniments for soaking up every last drop of the sauce.

SERVES 6

For the Chicken

1 white onion, peeled and cut into large chunks

3 cloves garlic, peeled and crushed with a mallet or the side of a knife

3 large sprigs fresh cilantro

6 boneless chicken breasts, with skin

6 cups light chicken broth (page 24)

Poaching the Chicken: In a large saucepan, combine the onion, garlic, cilantro and chicken. Cover with the broth, adding more broth or water if the chicken is not completely submerged. Bring to a simmer over medium-high heat. Reduce the heat to low and simmer until the chicken is tender, about 20 minutes. Remove from the heat.

For the Pepián Sauce

1/2 teaspoon cumin seeds

6-8 allspice berries

5 whole cloves

1/2 teaspoon black peppercorns

1 cup pepitas (green pumpkin seeds), unsalted

1/4 cup sesame seeds

1/2 cup peanuts, unskinned and unsalted

1 pound tomatillos (about 18 small to medium), husks removed, washed and coarsely chopped

1 white onion, peeled and coarsely chopped

2 cloves garlic, peeled and coarsely chopped

4-6 chiles serranos (about 2 inches each), stemmed and coarsely chopped

4 chiles poblanos, stems, seeds and membranes removed, coarsely chopped

1 cup romaine lettuce leaves, coarsely chopped

2 cups fresh cilantro, coarsely chopped

2 tablespoons mixed oil (see page 15)

1 teaspoon salt, or to taste

Garnish: Fresh cilantro sprigs

Preparing the Pepián Sauce: Pulverize the cumin, allspice, cloves and peppercorns in a spice/coffee grinder and set aside. Heat a large skillet over medium-high heat. When hot, toast the pepitas, stirring occasionally until they fatten and start to crackle, but are not brown, 3-4 minutes. Transfer to a medium bowl. In the same skillet, toast the sesame seeds, stirring occasionally, until they are light brown, 2-3 minutes. Transfer the seeds to the bowl and toast the peanuts in the same manner until they have a nice toasted color and flavor, about 3 minutes. Transfer the peanuts and pulverized spices to the bowl and toss to mix. In small batches, coarsely grind the seed mixture in a spice/coffee grinder. Do not over-process, or the resulting sauce will not have a rustic coarseness. Set aside the pulverized nuts and seeds.

Remove the poached chicken from the broth, remove the skin from the chicken and set aside the meat. Strain the broth through a sieve. Reserve 4 cups of broth, saving the rest for another use. Add 1/2 cup of the broth to the pulverized nuts and seeds and combine to make a coarse paste.

In a large bowl, combine the tomatillos, onion, garlic, chiles, romaine and cilantro. Toss to evenly mix. Transfer the tomatillo mixture to a blender in 3 batches and purée each batch with 1/2 cup of the reserved chicken broth until smooth. Set the purée aside in one bowl.

In a Dutch oven or large skillet, heat the oil over medium-high heat. When hot, add the pulverized nuts and seeds, and sauté until the mixture browns a bit, 4-5 minutes. Add the tomatillo purée, stir and cook for 2-3 minutes. Stir in the remaining 2 cups of chicken broth. The sauce should be quite watery. If it is not, stir in more broth. Reduce the heat to very low and simmer the mixture for 30 minutes. Add more broth during this time if the sauce becomes too thick to generously coat a spoon. Add the chicken breasts, cover with the sauce and continue to simmer until the chicken is heated through, about 10 minutes. Serve the chicken with additional sauce generously spooned on top. Garnish with sprigs of cilantro.

Veracruz-Style Red Snapper With Olives & Chiles

PESCADO A LA VERACRUZANA

This dish blends elements that are quintessentially Mexican and Spanish. The two sauces prepared for the recipe, the Mexican "Chiltomate"—meaning sauce of tomatoes and chiles—and the Spanish sauce of tomatoes, capers and olives, are cooked separately. It is in this manner that they develop their own flavors on their own terms. At the last moment before serving with the broiled red snapper, the two sauces are joined in a glorified marriage of flavor, better together than alone. Serve the fish and its flavorful sauce on a bed of Arroz Blanco (page 110). To serve as a first course, use 3-ounce fillets per portion.

SERVES 4 TO 8

For Advance Preparation
1 recipe Pickled Jalapeños (page 36)

For the Marinade
4 tablespoons extra virgin olive oil
2 tablespoons fresh lime juice
4 cloves garlic, peeled and minced
4 teaspoons dried Mexican oregano, slightly toasted
1 teaspoon freshly ground black pepper
1 teaspoon salt

4 red snapper fillets, or other mild, thick-fleshed fish, about 6 ounces each

Marinating the Fish: In a small bowl, mix the marinade ingredients with a fork. Rinse the fish and pat dry. Pluck the bones out with tweezers. Place the fillets in a large, non-metallic baking dish. Pour the marinade evenly over the top of the fillets. Turn to coat, rubbing the marinade into the flesh on both sides. The fish should just begin to turn opaque from the acidity of the lime juice. If it does not, squeeze a little more lime over the top. Cover the dish and let marinate in the refrigerator for 1 hour.

For the Chiltomate Sauce

2 plum tomatoes, peeled, seeded (see Techniques, page 19) and coarsely chopped

1/2 white onion, peeled and coarsely chopped

2 cloves garlic, peeled and coarsely chopped

2 tablespoons safflower oil

1/4 teaspoon dried marjoram

1/4 teaspoon dried thyme

2 small bay leaves, torn in half

1/2 cup light chicken broth (page 24), or canned broth

4 prepared Pickled Jalapeños, stems, seeds and membranes removed, cut into thin strips

2-3 tablespoons pickling juice from the prepared Pickled Jalapeños

Preparing the Chiltomate Sauce: Purée the tomatoes, onion and garlic in a blender. Heat the oil in a medium skillet over medium-high heat. When very hot, add the purée and sauté for 3 minutes. Add the marjoram, thyme and bay leaves and stir to mix. Stir in the broth, chiles and pickling juice, and bring to a boil. Cover, reduce the heat to very low and simmer for 15 minutes. The sauce should be the consistency of tomato sauce. If it is not, uncover and cook to reduce a little. Set aside.

For the Tomato-Olive Sauce

2 tablespoons capers

16 large green olives, pitted and chopped

1 tablespoon safflower oil

1/2 white onion, peeled and finely chopped

4 cloves garlic, minced

2 whole cloves

A 1/4-inch piece canela

1/4 teaspoon dried marjoram

1/4 teaspoon dried thyme

1 teaspoon dried Mexican oregano

1 bay leaf, torn in half

6 plum tomatoes, peeled, seeded (see Techniques, page 19) and coarsely chopped

Preparing the Tomato-Olive Sauce: In a small dish, mix the capers and olives, and set aside. In a large skillet, heat the oil over medium-high heat. Add the onion and garlic and sauté until soft but not brown, 3-4 minutes. In a spice/coffee grinder, pulverize the cloves and canela into a fine powder. Add the ground spices, marjoram, thyme, oregano and bay leaf to the skillet. Stir to mix and cook for about 1 minute. Add the tomatoes and 3/4 of the caper/olive mixture, reserving the rest for garnish. Stir to mix and sauté until dry. Add 1/2 cup of cold water, turn the heat to very low and simmer for 15 minutes. The sauce should be well-cooked to blend the flavors while remaining slightly chunky.

For Assembly
1/4 teaspoon freshly ground black pepper, or to taste
1/2 teaspoon salt, or to taste

Garnish: Pickled vegetables and chiles from the prepared Pickled Jalapeños

Assembling the Dish: Preheat the broiler to 500°F and adjust the oven rack to the highest notch. Mix the Chiltomate and Tomato-Olive sauces together in a single skillet. Stir to mix and remove from the heat. Taste for pepper and salt, making adjustments as necessary. Remove the fillets from their marinade and place them in a large, clean, non-metallic baking dish. Baste the tops with the juice from the combined sauce. Make sure the broiler is very hot and place the fish in the oven. Cook until the fish flakes easily with a fork, 5-7 minutes.

Reheat the sauce if necessary. If serving with rice, place a serving of rice on each plate and evenly divide the sauce over the rice, making tomato beds for the fillets. Place the fish on top and sprinkle with the reserved caper/olive mixture. Garnish with the pickled vegetables and chiles.

Tender Baked Fish in Banana Leaves

This dish features the flavors of the Yucatán. The smoky green flavor of banana leaves marries well with the astringent achiote, making the resulting tender fish a delectable treat. Banana leaves can be found frozen in many Mexican and Asian markets, but if they are not available, use kitchen parchment paper (see Cooking Notes below). If you must, use foil, but remove it before serving. For a tantalizing array of colors on the plate, accompany this dish with Arroz a la Mexicana (page 112) and Chipotle Salsa (page 41).

For the best flavor, make the achiote paste for the marinade the night before to allow it to develop its flavors. In the morning, dress the fish and marinate all day until cooking time.

SERVES 4

For Advance Preparation

1 recipe Yucatecan Achiote Paste (page 21)

2 recipes bitter orange juice (page 20)

1/2 pound frozen banana leaves, thawed overnight and prepared (see Techniques, page 17), torn into 4 pieces about 12 inches square, plus 1/4-inch wide strips for tying, and extra pieces for patching tears

For the Marinade

6 cloves garlic, roasted (see Techniques, page 19) and peeled

3 tablespoons prepared Yucatecan Achiote Paste

5 tablespoons prepared bitter orange juice

2 teaspoons dried Mexican oregano

1 teaspoon freshly ground black pepper

1/4 teaspoon salt

4 fillets of bass, halibut or other firm, very thick-fleshed fish, about 6 ounces each

Marinating the Fish: Mash the peeled garlic on a flat surface with the back of a fork. Scrape it up and transfer to a small bowl. Add the rest of the marinade ingredients and mix well, mashing with the fork to combine. Pluck the bones from the fish fillets with tweezers. Cut 3-4 diagonal slashes on the top of each fillet. Place the fillets in a single layer in a non-metallic baking dish. Pour half of the marinade over the fish and rub into the slashes. Turn over the fillets, rub the remaining marinade into the flesh and cover. Marinate in the refrigerator for 6-8 hours. If you are in a hurry, marinate at room temperature for 1 hour.

For the Pibil Parcels

2 tablespoons mixed oil (see page 15)

1/2 large red onion, peeled and sliced into 1/8-inch thick half moons

3 chiles güeros (or Anaheim or Hungarian wax), roasted and cut into rajas (see Techniques, page 18)

1/4 teaspoon dried marjoram

1/4 teaspoon dried thyme

2 tablespoons prepared bitter orange juice

2 tablespoons extra virgin olive oil

8 bay leaves

Garnish: 1 quartered lime and 4 tablespoons red onion, finely chopped

Preparing the Pibil Parcels: In a medium skillet, heat the oil over medium-high heat. When hot, add the onion and sauté until soft but not brown, 3-4 minutes. Add the rajas, marjoram and thyme. Stir to combine and continue to sauté until the onions are slightly brown, 3-5 minutes. Set aside.

Preheat the oven to 350°F. Remove the fish fillets from the marinade onto a plate. Mix the marinade with the bitter orange juice and olive oil and set aside. Prepare the banana leaves, as instructed in Techniques, or parchment paper (see Cooking Notes below). Lay a 12-inch square banana leaf, shiny side up, or the parchment paper on a flat work surface. If the banana leaf is torn in spots, cover the tears with extra leaf pieces. Place 1/8 of the cooked onions in the center of the banana leaf and top with 1 bay leaf and a fish fillet. Top with 1/4 of the marinade, another 1/8 portion of onions and 1 more bay leaf. Cross two of the banana leaf flaps over the fish and fold the remaining ends into an overlap, forming a snug packet. Secure in place with string or strips of banana leaf. Repeat for the remaining fillets and place the packets seam side up in a baking dish. Bake for 25 minutes. Remove the fish packets to plates or a serving platter. Fold back the edges of the banana leaves and curl them under the fish, making an attractive display. Garnish with a sprinkling of red onion on top and lime wedges on the side.

Cooking Notes

Preparing Parchment Packets (En Papillote): Tear off 4 sheets of kitchen parchment paper measuring 12 1/2 x 16 inches. Fold each piece in half to 12 1/2 x 8 inches. Drawing on kindergarten experience, cut out a half heart shape, so that the paper unfolds into a whole heart. Brush the outside of the parchment with oil. Place the ingredients on one side of the heart and fold over the other side to enclose it. Beginning at the top of the heart, fold the edge over once and then again, continuing to the bottom, creating a rope-style edge. When you reach the bottom of the heart, give it a twist to seal. Bake the parchment packets until puffed and brown, 20-25 minutes. Remove the packets to serving plates, slit open and pull the parchment back to reveal the fish. Garnish and serve.

Grilled Prawns in Achiote Citrus Marinade

CAMERONES EN ALAMBRES ACHIOTE

Close your eyes and imagine yourself on a beach in the Yucatán, aside a campfire that has burned to a bed of perfect coals, ready to impart a smoky flavor to marinated prawn skewers. The achiote paste and citrus juices in this recipe will caramelize in the grilling process, producing succulent, highly flavored prawns. For the best flavor, use the freshest prawns available and marinate them overnight. Serve the grilled prawns as an appetizer, or as an entrée crowning a mound of Arroz a la Mexicana (page 112) and topped with Pickled Red Onions (page 35). Finish with a dessert of Guavas and Pears in Syrup with Creamy Islands (page 120).

SERVES 6 ♦ YIELDS 12 SKEWERS

For Advance Preparation
1/2 recipe Yucatecan Achiote Paste (page 21)

1 cup orange juice

4 cloves garlic, peeled and halved

1/4 cup fresh lime juice (about 2 limes)

1 tablespoon cider vinegar

2 tablespoons prepared Yucatecan Achiote Paste

1 tablespoon honey or sugar

1/2 white onion, peeled and coarsely chopped

1 chile jalapeño, stem, seeds and membranes removed, coarsely chopped

2 tablespoons mixed oil (see page 15)

A large pinch of salt

3 pounds extra-large prawns (approximately 40), peeled (leave tails on) and deveined

12 bamboo skewers, soaked in water

Garnish: Fresh cilantro (leaves only)

In a medium skillet, heat the orange juice over medium-high heat, reduce to 1/3 cup and transfer to a blender. Add the garlic, lime juice, vinegar, achiote paste, honey, onion, chile and 2 tablespoons of water. Purée into a smooth marinade.

In a medium saucepan, heat the oil over medium-high heat. When hot, add the purée, bring to a simmer and cook until it darkens and thickens, 3-4 minutes. Remove from the heat and allow to cool. In a medium, non-metallic bowl, combine the marinade with the prawns and coat thoroughly. Cover and marinate in the refrigerator for 4 hours or overnight.

Thread the prawns on the softened bamboo skewers. Grill or broil the skewers 3 inches from the heat until the prawns are pink and curled, 2-3 minutes per side. Do not overcook. Serve the prawn skewers sprinkled with cilantro leaves.

THE JUAREZ MARKET IN MEXICO CITY OFFERS
DELIGHTFUL "AGUAS FRESCAS,"
OR REFRESHING DRINKS. THIS JAR, FILLED
WITH THE JUICE OF RIPE, SWEET PINEAPPLES,
MAKES AN EYE-CATCHING DISPLAY NESTLED IN
VERITABLE ICEBERGS.

Eggs With Rajas & Epazote

RABO DE MESTIZO

Comfort food! No matter your pride as a connoisseur of delicacies from around the world, there is always a food that is the subject of craving. When Monica, the daughter of our Pueblan guide, was asked about her favorite dish, her eyes lit up, and what she described was not a famous regional specialty. Instead, it was this simple egg dish. For a truly satisfying Mexican breakfast, serve with Beans in Broth (page 114), Arroz a la Mexicana (page 112), Corn Tortillas (page 106) and Pickled Jalapeños (page 36).

SERVES 6

6 plum tomatoes, roasted (see Techniques, page 19)

5 cloves garlic, peeled

1 white onion, peeled and sliced into thin half moons

2 tablespoon mixed oil (see page 15)

4 chiles poblanos, roasted and cut into rajas (see Techniques, page 18)

1 cup light chicken broth (page 24)

5 teaspoons dried epazote (leaves only)

1/2 teaspoon freshly ground black pepper

1/2-3/4 teaspoon salt, to taste

6 eggs

In a blender, purée the tomatoes, garlic and 1/4 of the onion. Set aside. Heat the oil in a large skillet over medium-high heat. Sauté the remaining onion and the rajas, stirring frequently, until the onion browns, about 5 minutes. Reduce the heat to medium, stir in the purée and bring to a boil. Cook until slightly thickened, about 3 minutes. Stir in the broth, epazote, pepper and salt, return to a boil and cook for 3 minutes. If the sauce becomes thick, stir in a little more broth or water to loosen it. Crack the eggs over the sauce, cover the skillet and poach the eggs until the whites are firm but the yolks are still soft, 3-5 minutes. Serve piping hot over rice.

Vegetable Entrées
& Side Dishes

Chayotes Stuffed With Tomatoes & Herbs

CHAYOTES CON JITOMATE Y HIERBAS

The chayote is a curious-looking vegetable, sometimes referred to as a vegetable pear. It grows on a vine and is frequently cultivated in Mexican kitchen gardens. It has a mellow flavor that picks up sweet or savory accents with ease, lending itself very nicely to stuffing. This recipe may be served as a first course, a sort of warm salad before a main course such as the Roast Pork Loin in Adobo (page 72). It also stands on its own as a light and healthy lunch entrée.

SERVES 4 TO 8

For the Chayote Shells

4 chayotes (about 10 1/2 ounces each)

1 tablespoon extra virgin olive oil

1 clove garlic, peeled

Freshly ground black pepper, to taste

Salt, to taste

Preparing the Chayote Shells: Place the chayotes in a large saucepan and cover them with cold water to about 1 inch above their surface. Cover the pan and bring to a boil over high heat. Reduce the heat to low and simmer partially covered until the chayotes are fork-tender, about 40 minutes. Drain the chayotes, rinse with cold water once or twice to stop the cooking and set aside to cool. When cool enough to handle, cut the chayotes in half lengthwise. Discard the seed and scoop out the pulp with a spoon or melon baller, leaving 1/4- to 1/2-inch thick walls remaining on the shell. Coarsely chop the pulp and set aside.

Although the peel of the chayote can be eaten, the texture of the dish is nicer if the skin is removed with a vegetable peeler. Do not peel too much skin, especially around the cut edges, or the shell will pull apart, losing some of its presentation value. Place the shells in a large baking dish, cut side down, and set aside. In a small skillet, heat the olive oil over medium heat. When hot, add the garlic clove and sauté until golden, about 3 minutes. Remove the garlic from the skillet and brush the infused oil on the chayote shells. Sprinkle with pepper and salt. Turn over the shells and repeat the process. Leave the cut sides up in the baking dish and set aside.

For the Chayote Stuffing
1 tablespoon mixed oil (see page 15)
1/2 white onion, peeled and finely chopped
2 cloves garlic, peeled and minced
4 plum tomatoes, peeled, seeded (see Techniques, page 19) and finely chopped
1 teaspoon dried marjoram
2 teaspoons dried Mexican oregano
1/2 teaspoon freshly ground black pepper
1/2 teaspoon salt
1/4 cup dried bread crumbs
1/4 cup queso fresco, or mild feta cheese, crumbled

Garnish: 2 tablespoons flat-leaf parsley leaves, coarsely chopped

Stuffing and Baking the Chayotes: Preheat the oven to 375°F. In a medium skillet, heat the oil over medium-high heat. When hot, add the onion and sauté just until it begins to brown, about 5 minutes. Add the garlic and sauté for 2 minutes. Add the tomatoes, marjoram, oregano, pepper and salt. Stir and cook for 2 more minutes. Stir in the bread crumbs and mix well. Remove the skillet from the heat and mix in the chayote pulp until evenly combined with the tomato mixture. Fill each chayote shell with the stuffing and top with cheese. Bake uncovered until the cheese is melted and the chayotes are heated through, 10-15 minutes. Top each stuffed chayote with a sprinkling of parsley and serve.

Pueblan Five Vegetable Green Mole

MOLE VERDE DE PUEBLA

This recipe is an unusual vegetarian version of a mole verde particular to Puebla. In fact, it doesn't bear any resemblance to the moles verdes found in other regions of Mexico, which are more similar to Puebla's Pepián Verde (see Chicken in Green Pumpkin Seed Sauce, page 81). Mónica Mastretta Tiburcio, a friend and guide in Puebla, described this recipe by stating that the only requirement is to include five different green vegetables. Generally, fresh fava beans are used instead of lima beans. If they are in season, try them, but be sure to remove the pods and boil the beans until the bitter outer skins are soft enough to remove before adding them to the pan. Serve this mole verde with rice for a nice healthy supper, or as a side dish with pork, such as Soft Tacos with Yucatán-Style Shredded Pork (page 64) or Tamales with Shredded Pork and Chile Guajillo (page 53).

SERVES 6

4 allspice berries

A 1/2-inch piece canela

1 tablespoon mixed oil (see page 15)

1/4 white onion, peeled and chopped

2 cloves garlic, peeled and chopped

1/2 pound tomatillos, husks removed, washed and quartered

3 chiles serranos (about 2 inches each), stemmed, quartered lengthwise, seeds and membranes removed, coarsely chopped

1 small or 1/2 large romaine leaf, or 1 iceberg lettuce leaf, torn into pieces

4 radish leaves

4 cups vegetable or light chicken broth (page 26 or 24)

1 medium chayote, peeled, seeded and cut into 1-inch cubes

2 zucchini, ends trimmed and cut into 1/2-inch cubes

1/4 pound green beans, trimmed and cut into 1 1/2-inch pieces

1/2 cup frozen lima beans, thawed

1/2 cup frozen peas, thawed

1/2 cup fresh cilantro (leaves only), roughly chopped

1/4 teaspoon freshly ground black pepper

1/4 teaspoon salt, or to taste

Garnish: *1/4 cup queso añejo, or parmesan cheese, grated*

In a spice/coffee grinder, pulverize the allspice and canela into a fine powder and set aside. In a large, thick-sided saucepan, heat the oil over medium-high heat. When hot, add the onion and sauté until soft, 3-4 minutes. Add the garlic, tomatillos and chiles. Sauté, stirring frequently, until the tomatillos turn soft and golden, about 5 minutes. Stir in the pulverized spices, lettuce and radish leaves and sauté until the lettuce wilts, about 2 minutes. Transfer the mixture to a blender with 1/2 cup of the broth and purée. Return the purée to the pan and add the remaining broth. Bring to a boil, reduce the heat to low and simmer uncovered for 20 minutes. Skim the surface with a large spoon if a skin forms during this time.

Stir in the chayote, zucchini and green beans. Increase the heat to medium-high and bring the mixture back to a simmer. Reduce the heat to low and simmer for 20 more minutes. Add the lima beans and peas and simmer for 10 minutes. Stir in the cilantro, pepper and salt. Taste for balance of flavor, making adjustments to the salt as necessary. Serve hot or at room temperature, with a sprinkling of cheese on top.

Chile Chipotle Grilled Vegetables

VERDURAS A LAS BRASAS DE CHILE CHIPOTLE

There is nothing better on a warm summer evening than a stunning display of bounty from the barbecue. In this recipe, the intoxicating aroma of grilled corn and chile chipotle will keep plates headed your way. Vegetarian friends will especially appreciate this delicious barbecue experience. A squeeze of lime is the only finish required to serve the vegetables. When preparing to make this dish, start at your local produce or farmers' market to select the freshest ingredients. Feel free to mix in other vegetables or even fruits, such as pineapple. The vegetables may be grilled or roasted. Accompany with Black Bean and Corn Salsa (page 40) and perhaps a nice Roasted Beef Tenderloin (page 76).

SERVES 4 TO 6

2 tablespoons mixed oil (see page 15)

1 chile chipotle, fried (see Techniques, page 17)

1 chile ancho, fried (see Techniques, page 17)

1 large sweet potato or yam (about 3/4 pound), peeled

2 large ears yellow corn, husks removed, trimmed and cut into 1 1/2-inch rounds

2 large red bell peppers, stems, seeds and membranes removed, each cut into 6 strips

6 medium green summer squash (about 1 pound), cut in half to form rounds

8 baby leeks, or green onions, ends trimmed

2 cloves garlic, peeled and coarsely chopped

1 tablespoon fresh lime juice

2 tablespoons rice vinegar

A 1/2-inch piece canela, ground

1/4 teaspoon freshly ground black pepper

1/2 teaspoon salt

Garnish: Fresh cilantro sprigs, lime wedges, crema Mexicana (page 20)

Using the oil, prepare the chiles as instructed in Techniques and reserve the oil. Soak the chiles for 30 minutes. Cut the sweet potato into 1-inch thick slices. Cut the slices in half to form half moons, transfer to a medium saucepan, cover with water and bring to a simmer over medium-high heat. Reduce the heat to low and simmer until fork-tender, about 8 minutes. Drain and set aside to cool. Place the sweet potatoes and corn in one bowl, and the red peppers, squash and leeks in another bowl.

To prepare the marinade, drain the chiles and transfer to a blender with 6 tablespoons of the soaking liquid. Add the garlic, lime juice, vinegar, canela, pepper, salt and the reserved oil from frying the chiles, and purée into a smooth, thick marinade. Divide the marinade between the bowls of vegetables and toss to coat evenly. Marinate for 30 minutes before grilling.

Prepare the grill and preheat the oven to 200°F. When the coals are ready (you'll be able to hold your hand at grill level for only 3-4 seconds), brush the grill rack with oil. Grill the sweet potatoes and corn, turning until lightly browned on all sides, 10-15 minutes. Remove the vegetables to a baking pan, cover and keep warm in the oven. Grill the red peppers, squash and leeks, 5-7 minutes.

Alternatively, to broil the vegetables, preheat the broiler to 500°F. Place the sweet potatoes and corn in a roasting pan 3 inches from the heat and roast for 10 minutes on each side. Remove from the pan and keep covered. Add the red peppers, squash and leeks to the roasting pan and roast, turning once, until cooked through, 5-10 minutes.

Arrange the roasted vegetables on a serving platter, grouping like vegetables together. Drizzle crema Mexicana in a thin stream over the vegetables. Squeeze several wedges of lime over the top and garnish with sprigs of cilantro and more wedges of lime.

Green Chiles Rellenos Stuffed With Butternut Squash

CHILES RELLENOS DE CALABAZA

This recipe uses the readily available butternut squash in place of the "cal-abaza," or pumpkin, which is the squash of choice in Mexico. The sweet, earthy flavor and bright orange color of the butternut squash make it an appealing complement to the roasted green chile poblano. The squash filling without the cheese also works as a rich and colorful side dish. For an impressive vegetarian meal, accompany the rellenos with Beans in Broth (page 114) and Pickled Green Cabbage Relish (page 38), and finish with a dessert of Jamaica "Flower" and Raspberry Sorbet (page 124).

SERVES 4 TO 8

For the Butternut Squash Filling

1 small butternut squash (about 1 pound), peeled, cored and cut into 1/4-inch cubes (see Cooking Notes below)

4 teaspoons extra virgin olive oil

1/4 teaspoon freshly ground black pepper, or to taste

1/4 teaspoon salt, or to taste

3 cloves garlic, peeled and minced

1 teaspoon dried Mexican oregano

3 tablespoons pine nuts, toasted

2 tablespoons flat-leaf parsley leaves, coarsely chopped

3 tablespoons queso fresco, or mild feta cheese, crumbled

Preparing the Filling: Preheat the broiler to 500°F and adjust the oven rack to the highest notch. Place the cubed squash in a bowl and toss with 2 teaspoons of the oil, the pepper and salt. Spread the squash in a single layer in a roasting pan and roast for 20 minutes, turning with a spatula after 10 minutes. Remove the squash from the oven, set aside and reduce the oven temperature to 350°F.

Heat the remaining oil in a large skillet over medium heat. Add the garlic and sauté until golden, 2-3 minutes. Add the oregano, roasted squash and pine nuts. Stir gently to combine all of the ingredients, taste for salt and adjust if necessary. Stir in the parsley and cheese and remove from the heat.

For the Chiles Rellenos

8 chiles poblanos, roasted and prepared for rellenos (see Techniques, page 18)

1/3 cup crema Mexicana (page 20), drizzling consistency

Garnish: 8 fresh flat-leaf parsley sprigs

Stuffing and Baking the Chiles: Spoon the filling into the opening of each chile, filling the crevices, yet allowing the opening to be fully closed over the filling. Place the chiles seam side down in a baking pan, side by side, and cover with foil. Bake until heated through, 15-20 minutes. To serve, place 1-2 chiles on a plate, drizzle with crema Mexicana and garnish with parsley sprigs.

Cooking Notes

Easy Squash Peeling Method: To peel the butternut squash (or any thick-skinned, rounded vegetable or fruit), start by trimming the top and bottom. For pear-shaped vegetables like the butternut squash, cut into two pieces at the area transitioning from the thin neck to the wide belly. Place the flat end of one piece on a work surface. With a paring knife, remove the peel in vertical strips from top to bottom. Work the knife around the circumference of the squash, peeling off strips in sequential movement.

Sweet Potato & Black Bean Picadillo

"Camotes," or sweet potatoes, are a favorite Mexican treat. In this recipe, the flavor of the root is highlighted by raisins. Use this preparation as a side dish, to fill quesadillas or to stuff chiles rellenos, either green chiles poblanos (page 100) or dried, red chiles anchos (page 73). The Jicama, Pineapple and Watercress Salad (page 34) is a beautiful side dish that complements the sweet potatoes with an astringent, sweet and sour flavor. The filling may be made a day ahead and reheated before using.

YIELDS STUFFING FOR 8 CHILES RELLENOS

For Advance Preparation

3/4 cup Oaxacan-Style Beans in Broth (page 115), or canned black beans, drained

1 sweet potato (about 8 ounces), peeled

1 chile chipotle, stem, seeds and membranes removed

1/2 cup raisins

1/4 cup orange juice

1/2 white onion, peeled and coarsely chopped

3 cloves garlic, peeled and crushed with a mallet or the side of a knife

3 plum tomatoes, seeded (see Techniques, page 19) and quartered

2 whole cloves

A 1-inch piece canela

1/4 teaspoon black peppercorns

1 tablespoon mixed oil (see page 15)

1/3 cup blanched slivered almonds, toasted and coarsely chopped

2 teaspoons cider vinegar

1/4 teaspoon freshly ground black pepper

1/2 teaspoon salt

Cut the sweet potato into 3 large pieces. Place in a medium saucepan, cover with water and bring to a boil over medium-high heat. Reduce the heat to low and simmer until fork-tender, about 25 minutes. Drain, allow to cool a little and cut into 1/4-inch cubes. Set aside.

Place the chile chipotle in a small bowl, cover with about 3/4 cup water at its boiling point and soak for 30 minutes. In a small bowl, soak the raisins in the orange juice until softened, about 20 minutes. Place the onion, garlic and tomatoes in a blender and set aside. Place the cloves, canela and peppercorns in a spice/coffee grinder, pulverize into a powder and add to the blender.

Drain the chile, reserving 1/2 cup of the soaking liquid. Add the chile and reserved soaking liquid to the blender. Purée the tomato/chipotle mixture into a smooth sauce. Heat the oil in a large skillet over medium-high heat. When very hot, add the sauce and sauté until it has thickened a little, about 5 minutes. Add the sweet potato, black beans, almonds and soaked raisins and continue cooking until the mixture is dry. Season with the vinegar, pepper and salt, stir to combine, and taste for balance of flavor. Serve hot as a side dish, or set aside to cool before using as a filling.

Swiss Chard Filling

The earthy flavor of the hardy Swiss chard combines well with the sweetness of canela and orange juice, making this dish a delicious vegetarian filling for quesadillas (page 68) or tamales (pages 53-59). It also makes a tasty and interesting accompaniment to Roasted Beef Tenderloin (page 76).

YIELDS 2 CUPS

1 pound Swiss chard

2 teaspoons mixed oil (see page 15)

1/8 white onion, peeled and finely chopped

2 cloves garlic, peeled and minced

A 3/8-inch piece canela, ground

2 chiles serranos (about 2 inches each), stems, seeds and membranes removed, minced

1/2 cup orange juice

2 plum tomatoes, seeded (see Techniques, page 19) and finely chopped

3/8 teaspoon salt

Garnish: 2 tablespoons queso añejo, or parmesan cheese, grated (optional)

Immerse the chard in water, allowing any sand to drop to the bottom of the sink or bowl. Rinse each leaf. Tear away the dark green parts from the white stalks in large pieces. Set aside. Trim the stalks, chop very finely and reserve 1 1/4 cups, saving the rest for another use. In a medium skillet, heat the oil over medium-high heat. When hot, add the onion and sauté until brown, about 5 minutes. Stir in the garlic, canela, chiles, chopped stalks and if dry, a little of the juice. Sauté until the chiles turn bright green, about 2 minutes. Stir in the tomatoes and the remaining juice. Cover the skillet, reduce the heat to medium and cook for 3 minutes. Lay the chard leaves over the tomatoes, cover and cook until the leaves wilt, about 5 minutes. Stir the mixture and reduce over high heat until moist but not runny, about 5 minutes. Stir in the salt, garnish and serve hot.

Corn Tortillas

TORTILLAS DE MAÍZ

Tortillas are the staple of every Mexican meal. The traditional method of pressing out tortillas is by hand. It is an amazing thing to see, and if you have a "papuseria" or an old-fashioned tortilla factory in your area, as we do in the Mission district of San Francisco, you can watch the ladies dexterously pat out the dough. Most homemade tortillas are made with a tortilla press, but you can use a rolling pin. When purchasing masa harina, be aware that the brand is very important. Some brands retain the lime from processing, causing the dough to turn an unsavory white color and taste bad. For the best results, purchase Quaker or Maseca brand masa harina, available at Mexican markets and some supermarkets.

YIELDS 16 TORTILLAS, 5 1/2 INCHES IN DIAMETER

1 3/4 cups masa harina

1/8 teaspoon salt

1 cup warm water, plus 1/3 cup in reserve

In a medium bowl, stir together the masa harina and salt. Using your hands, mix in the 1 cup of warm water. Knead the dough until the flour and water are well combined. The dough should be very pliable, like soft taffy, and its surface should be just slightly tacky without actually sticking to your hands. As you knead and pull on the dough in the bowl, it will sound like very soft Velcro. Add the water in reserve, 1 tablespoon at a time, until this texture is achieved. Cover the dough with a damp towel and let stand for 30 minutes.

Divide the dough in half, and then each half into 8 balls, about 1 1/2 inches in diameter. Keep the dough balls covered as you work so they stay moist. Cut 2 large pieces of heavy plastic about 6-7 inches square. A Ziploc bag is handy for this—just cut off the closure and snip at the seams. Place a dough ball between the plastic sheets and press down gently with your palm to flatten it a little. If you have a tortilla press, place the dough ball and its plastic envelope in the center of the press and firmly push down the handle, being careful not to push too hard, or the tortilla will be too thin to handle without tearing. If you are using a rolling pin, keep the dough ball between the plastic sheets and roll to flatten into a 3-inch disk. Then roll out the dough from its center, rotating 1/6 of a turn after each roll. Don't roll past the edges or the tortilla will be too thin. Work quickly to form evenly thick, round tortillas about 5 1/2 inches in diameter. Don't be too devastated if it takes some practice to roll out perfect rounds, but refrain from over-rolling, or the tortilla will not puff up when cooked.

Preheat the oven to 200°F. Set a clean towel on a plate to wrap the tortillas as they finish cooking. Heat a dry medium non-stick skillet over medium-high heat. Pull the top piece of plastic off the rolled-out tortilla by pulling it directly back, not up. Turn the tortilla onto your hand and pull off the second sheet of plastic in the same manner. Using both sets of fingers—not your palms, as the dough has a tendency to stick—drape the tortilla flat into the skillet. Cook until the tortilla can be released from the skillet with a spatula, about 20 seconds. Flip the tortilla and cook until light brown spots start to appear on the bottom, about 1 minute. Flip the tortilla again—it should puff up. Cook for 20-30 seconds, remove to the towel-lined plate and cover. Continue in the same manner until all of the tortillas are cooked. To keep the tortillas warm before serving, wrap the stack, towel and all, in foil and place in the oven for up to an hour. Serve hot.

Cooking Notes

Storing and Reheating Tortillas: Wrap the tortillas tightly in foil and store in the refrigerator. Reheat the packet in a preheated 300°F oven for about 10 minutes. Alternatively, heat a dry skillet over medium-high heat, and warm the tortillas 3 at a time, flipping to heat each side.

Flour Tortillas

TORTILLAS DE HARINA

Tortillas are the bread of Mexico, and have been a source of sustenance for thousands of years. Flour tortillas are typical of northern Mexico, where corn will not grow. These tortillas are delicious fresh off the skillet and provide a nice alternative to bread with any meal. Try them as an accompaniment to Roasted Beef Tenderloin (page 76).

YIELDS 14 TORTILLAS, 5 1/2 INCHES IN DIAMETER

2 1/2 cups all-purpose flour

1 teaspoon salt

1/3 cup vegetable shortening, such as Crisco

3/4 cup warm water, plus 1-2 tablespoons in reserve

Combine the flour and salt in a large bowl and mix well. Using a fork, work the shortening into the flour until the mixture resembles corn meal. Make a well in the center of the flour mixture and pour in the water. Continue working with the fork until a ball begins to form. Knead the dough on a work surface, adding more flour if the dough is too sticky, until the dough is pliable and elastic. If the dough seems too dry, add the additional water, 1 teaspoon at a time, until the right consistency is achieved. Cover the dough with a damp towel and let stand for 30 minutes.

Divide the dough in half, and then each half into 7 small balls. Keep the dough balls covered as you work so they stay moist. Cut 2 large pieces of heavy plastic about 6-7 inches square. A Ziploc bag is handy for this—just cut off the closure and snip at the seams. Place a dough ball between the plastic sheets and press down gently with your palm to flatten it a little. If you have a tortilla press, place the dough ball and its plastic envelope in the center of the press and firmly push down the handle, being careful not to push too hard, or the tortilla will be too thin to handle without tearing. If you are using a rolling pin, keep the dough ball between the plastic sheets and roll out the dough from its center, rotating 1/6 of a turn after each roll. Work quickly to form evenly thick, round tortillas about 5 1/2 inches in diameter. Don't be too devastated if it takes some practice to roll out perfect rounds, but refrain from over-rolling, or the tortilla will not puff up when cooked.

Preheat the oven to 200°F. Set a clean towel on a plate to wrap the tortilla as they finish cooking. Heat a dry, medium, non-stick skillet over medium-high heat, add a tortilla and cook until it begins to bubble and puff, about 1 minute. Flip and cook the other side for 30 seconds. Both sides should be covered with brown flecks. Remove to the towel-lined plate and cover. Continue in the same manner until all of the tortillas are cooked. To keep the tortillas warm before serving, wrap the stack, towel and all, in foil and place in the oven for up to an hour. Serve hot. If not using immediately, see the Cooking Notes on page 107 for instructions on how to store and reheat tortillas.

THIS OAXACAN WOMAN IS MAKING
TORTILLAS ON A "COMAL" HEATED OVER AN
AROMATIC CEDAR FIRE.

Arroz Blanco

This rice is absolutely delicious and sure to please the rice lovers in your home. It pairs well with just about any of the recipes in this book, as well as many dishes you may already cook. The addition of fried plantain makes for a spectacular presentation. Cut a 4-inch length from a plantain or green banana and cut again into 4 lengthwise slices. Fry the pieces on both sides until attractively brown, and arrange them on top of the rice platter before serving.

SERVES 4 TO 6

2 cups long grain white rice (do not use an aromatic variety such as basmati)

6 cups water, at its boiling point

1 white onion, peeled, 1/2 coarsely chopped and 1/2 left in one piece

7 cloves garlic, peeled, 3 coarsely chopped and 4 left whole

4 tablespoons safflower oil

3/4 teaspoon salt, or to taste

3 whole chiles serranos (about 2 inches each) or chiles jalapeños

15 sprigs fresh flat-leaf parsley, stems removed and coarsely chopped

Place the rice in a fine-mesh strainer and rinse with cold running water. Transfer to a bowl, cover with 4 cups of the hot water and soak for 15 minutes. Pour off as much of the hot water as possible without losing grains. Rinse the rice again under cold running water, stirring with your hand and frequently pouring off the starch-clouded water. Drain well through a strainer and set aside.

In a blender, purée the chopped onion and garlic with 2 tablespoons of water, scraping the sides of the blender to evenly purée. It should measure about 1 cup. If it is more or less, you will need to adjust the amount of cooking water slightly. Set aside.

Heat the oil in a medium, thick-sided, preferably non-stick saucepan over medium-high heat. When hot, add the half piece of onion and the whole garlic. Sauté until the garlic begins to brown, about 3 minutes. Add the drained rice. Stir frequently until the grains turn golden brown, 10-12 minutes. Remove the pan from the heat and remove the onion and garlic pieces. Return the pan to the heat. Add the onion purée, stir to mix and cook until the onion mixture is completely absorbed, about 2 minutes. Add the remaining 2 cups of hot water and the salt, stirring once or twice to mix. Bring the mixture to a boil for 1 minute. Do not stir again. Lay the chiles and parsley over the top of the rice. Reduce the heat to very low, cover tightly and simmer until all of the liquid is absorbed and the rice is tender, about 15 minutes. Remove the pan from the heat, fluff the rice and test for texture (see Cooking Notes below), making adjustments if necessary. Cover again and let stand for 5 minutes. Spoon the rice onto a platter or bowl. Arrange the chiles and optional fried plantain pieces on top, and serve.

Cooking Notes

Steps to Perfect Rice: The first key to great rice is to use a thick-sided saucepan. A thin metal pan is guaranteed to burn the rice onto the bottom of the pan. Burnt rice transfers an unappealing carbon flavor to the unburned rice. If you do scald the rice, quickly remove the unburned portion to a dish so the carbon flavor does not set.

When you check the rice texture, it should be tender, not mushy, and definitely not al dente—hard to the tooth. If the rice is too soft, remove the cover and cook over low heat for a few minutes to evaporate excess moisture. If the rice is too hard and all the moisture has already been steamed into the rice, add 1 or 2 tablespoons of water, cover the pan and continue to cook over low heat until the water is absorbed and the texture is just right.

Arroz a la Mexicana

RICE WITH TOMATOES AND VEGETABLES

This is a typical Mexican rice dish that many Americans have enjoyed, either south of the border or in a neighborhood restaurant. The red color comes from tomatoes, not saffron as many people think. The rice is fried until golden before adding the liquid, enhancing the flavor of the rice and protecting it from mushiness. Whether served as part of a simple meal with beans, tortillas, a fried egg and a couple of Pickled Jalapeños (page 36), or with the elegant preparation of Grilled Prawns in Achiote Citrus Marinade (page 90), this rice dish is sure to make a colorful and tasty addition to the table. By the way, the chiles in this recipe do not add heat when left whole, they just look pretty and give off a little flavor from their skins. Simply warn guests not to eat them like pickles!

SERVES 4 TO 6

2 cups long grain white rice (do not use an aromatic variety such as basmati)

4 cups water, at its boiling point

3 plum tomatoes, seeded (see Techniques, page 19) and chopped

1/2 white onion, peeled and chopped

1 clove garlic, peeled and chopped

4 tablespoons mixed oil (see page 15)

3/4 teaspoon salt, or to taste

2 cups light chicken or vegetable broth (page 24 or 26)

Optional Vegetables:

1/2 cup carrot, peeled and thinly sliced on the diagonal, or other vegetables

2-3 whole chiles serranos (about 2 inches each)

Place the rice in a fine-mesh strainer and rinse with cold running water. Transfer to a bowl, cover with the hot water and soak for 15 minutes. Pour off as much of the hot water as possible without losing grains. Rinse the rice again under cold running water, stirring with your hand and frequently pouring off the starch-clouded water. Drain well through a strainer and set aside.

In a blender, purée the tomatoes, onion and garlic. Add a tablespoon of water, only if absolutely necessary to free the blades. There should be about 1 1/3 cups of tomato purée. If there is more, you will need to reduce the amount of broth a little.

Heat the oil in a medium, thick-sided, preferably non-stick saucepan over medium-high heat. When hot, add the rice and stir frequently until the grains turn golden brown, 10-12 minutes. Add the tomato purée and salt. Stir to mix and cook until the purée is absorbed, about 2 minutes. Add the broth and the optional carrot and chiles. Stir to mix and bring to a boil. Reduce the heat to very low, cover tightly and simmer until all the liquid is absorbed and the rice is tender, about 15 minutes. Remove the pan from the heat, fluff the rice and test for texture (see Cooking Notes, page 111). Taste for salt and make adjustments if necessary. Cover again and let stand for 5 minutes. Serve hot in a serving dish, or on individual plates, topped with the chiles for an attractive display.

THE CHARMING AVENIDA ALCALA IN
OAXACA IS FILLED WITH DELIGHTFUL SIGHTS.
THIS TRIO OF MUSICIANS SEEMS TO
BE COMMANDED BY THE SMALL BOY, WHO IS
STRUMMING A FISH.

Beans in Broth

FRIJOLES DE OLLA

After an eating tour of Puebla and Mexico City, where beans in broth were commonly served, none of us could quite understand the Mexican love for beans. That is, until we had them at a particular lunch in Mexico City. Those beans begged for a second serving. The secret to good beans, our hostess said, is to char a small bit of onion coal-black—it makes all the difference in this ubiquitous Mexican bean dish. Now you, too, know the secret to apply to the many variations of this simple recipe. Pinto beans are generally used for the dish, and a nice variation is to include aniseed, which adds a slightly sweet note. For a more savory bean dish, try Oaxacan-Style Beans in Broth, with black turtle beans and epazote (see below).

Whatever the bean or the flavorings used, Beans in Broth are always better on the second day, so prepare them a day in advance. Don't cut back on the salt for this dish—it brings out the full flavor of the beans.

SERVES 4 TO 6 ♦ YIELDS APPROXIMATELY 5 CUPS

1 1/3 cup pinto beans (about 1/2 pound)
1 tablespoon mixed oil (see page 15)
1/8 white onion, peeled and chopped
1/4 teaspoon aniseed, toasted and ground (optional)
5 cups water, at its boiling point
1-1 1/4 teaspoons salt

Immerse the beans in cold water, discard floating beans, drain and pick through, removing any small stones. Set aside—do not soak the beans! In a large saucepan, heat the oil over medium-high heat. When hot, add the onion and cook until it is burned coal-black throughout, 5-10 minutes. You may want to turn on the stove fan during this process. Add the beans, the optional aniseed and the hot water. Turn the heat to low, partially cover and continue to cook at a low boil until the skins have softened, about 50 minutes. Keep a separate small saucepan of hot water on low heat, and add to the beans if they start to poke out of their broth. Do not add the salt until the bean skins have already softened or they won't ever soften. Add the salt and continue to cook until the beans are very soft, but not disintegrating, 30-50 more minutes. The finished product should not be mushy, nor should it be al dente—hard to the tooth. Before serving, you may remove the charred onion if you wish.

Oaxacan-Style Beans in Broth

FRIJOLES DE OLLA A LA OAXAQUEÑA

YIELDS APPROXIMATELY 5 CUPS

To make this delicious dish, follow the methodology and quantities of ingredients above with the following exceptions: Use black beans in place of the pinto beans. Use 1 tablespoon dried, crumbled epazote leaves instead of the aniseed. Use 6 cups water at its boiling point. Cook the beans until you are certain the skins have softened, about 1 hour, before adding the salt. And finally, cook the beans until they are soft all the way through, but not mushy, about 1 more hour, or longer if the beans are old.

Refried Beans With Onion

FRIJOLES REFRITOS

These beans are not actually fried twice—a more accurate description would be well-cooked. Whatever the nomenclature, this recipe is made with Beans in Broth using pinto beans, or with the black bean version, Oaxacan-Style Beans in Broth (page 115). The two types of beans have different flavors, but they are equally delicious. You must try them both to discover your preference. The look and taste of homemade refried beans are quite different from the typical canned, or even restaurant, variety. They are a tasty and very enjoyable component of a well-prepared Mexican meal.

YIELDS APPROXIMATELY 1 3/4 CUPS

1 tablespoon mixed oil (see page 15)

1/8 white onion, peeled and minced

1/2 recipe Beans in Broth (page 114), about 2 cups undrained beans plus 1/2 cup broth

In a medium skillet, heat the oil over medium-high heat. When hot, add the onion and sauté until translucent but not brown, about 3 minutes. Add half of the beans, plus the additional broth, and stir to mix. With the skillet still on the heat, begin mashing the beans with a fork, potato masher or Mexican bean masher. Mash the beans, occasionally scraping them from the bottom of the skillet, until they are a fairly coarse purée and no whole beans remain, about 3 minutes. Add the remaining beans and work into the purée in the same manner. Add more broth, or water, if the mixture dries out too much. After all of the beans are mashed, continue to cook until you can see the bottom surface of the skillet as you stir, 5-7 minutes. Add the remaining broth or water liberally to maintain a thick, creamy texture before serving or using in another recipe. If using later, cool, cover and refrigerate.

Spiced Crêpes With Goat Milk Caramel

CREPAS DE CAJETA

"Cajeta," or goat milk caramel sauce, is very popular in Mexico. In addition to these crêpes, cajeta is incredibly good with vanilla ice cream. A curious variation is a candy, widely available in Mexican markets both here and in Mexico, in which the caramel is sandwiched between two very thin wafers. The wafers bear a remarkable resemblance to those served as Communion, and in fact the factory that supplies the church also supplies the candy shop. One benefit of the candy shop's cajeta addition is that the wafers don't stick to the roof of your mouth. Problem solved! Serve these crêpes to conclude an elegant menu.

SERVES 6 ♦ YIELDS 18 CRÊPES

For the Cajeta

1 cup orange juice

1/4 teaspoon baking soda

4 cups whole goat milk, or cow milk

1 cup sugar

1/2 tablespoon Grand Marnier, or brandy (optional)

Preparing the Cajeta: Bring the juice to a boil in a skillet over high heat. Reduce to 1/4 cup, transfer to a small bowl and cool. When cool, stir in the baking soda—it will foam up to twice the volume. In a large saucepan over medium-high heat, combine the milk and sugar and bring to a boil. Reduce the heat to low and stir in the orange juice mixture. Continue simmering, stirring frequently, until the mixture darkens to a pale amber color and thickens to coat the back of a spoon, about 40 minutes. Gentle bubbles will pop to the surface of the caramel during the last 10 minutes of cooking. If the sauce has not thickened, increase the heat and cook until thick. You should have about 1 cup of sauce. Remove from the heat and pour into a wide-mouthed jar to cool a little. Stir in the optional liqueur and cover. The sauce will keep in the refrigerator indefinitely.

For the Crêpes
2 eggs, lightly beaten
1 cup whole milk
1 tablespoon butter, melted
2/3 cup all-purpose flour
1/4 teaspoon salt
Zest of 1 orange (see Cooking Notes, page 121)
2 teaspoons sugar
A 1/2-inch piece canela, ground
Vegetable oil, for cooking crêpes

Garnish: 1/3-1/2 cup blanched slivered almonds, toasted and coarsely chopped

Preparing the Crêpes: Combine all of the crêpe ingredients, except the oil and garnish, in a blender. Purée into a batter the consistency of heavy cream, adding a little water if necessary. Let stand for 30 minutes.

Heat a large non-stick skillet or crêpe pan over medium heat. Brush lightly with oil. When hot, pour 2 tablespoons batter in the center of the skillet. Make a thin 6-inch disk by quickly swivelling the skillet around in a circle. Cook the crêpe until it is dry on top and nicely browned on the bottom, 45 seconds. Flip and cook another 20 seconds. Turn the crêpe onto a sheet of aluminum foil. Repeat the process, brushing more oil on the skillet as necessary, until all of the batter has been used. Stack the crêpes slightly off-center to more easily separate later. Cover with another sheet of foil and fold over the edges to create a packet. The crêpes may be made 1-2 days ahead and refrigerated.

Assembling the Dish: About 20 minutes prior to serving, preheat the oven to 350°F. Place the packet of crêpes in the oven and allow to heat through, about 10 minutes. Meanwhile, in a small saucepan over low to medium heat, gently warm the caramel sauce. To assemble the dish, fold each crêpe in half twice, forming lazy quarters. On a dessert plate, overlap 2-3 folded crêpes, spoon the warm caramel sauce over the crêpes and sprinkle with the almonds. Repeat with the remaining crêpes and serve warm.

Guavas & Pears in Syrup With Creamy Islands

GUAYABAS EN ALMÍBAR

The guavas used in this dish are the yellow variety. Indigenous to tropical areas, yellow guavas are used in cooked dishes. In contrast, green guavas with pink flesh are for eating fresh, not cooking. These yellow guavas in syrup make a classic Mexican dessert with an intriguing presentation. Each tart guava is cut in half, forming the perfect shell for a delicious lake of sweet amber syrup, finished with a creamy island of sour cream. If you are a fiend for metaphor, call them "Guayabas Aztecas" and equate this dessert to the urban design of Mexico City in the age of the Aztecs, a lake city surrounded by mountains, traversed by canals as roads and byways. However, if you just want to think about dessert, this one is simple to make and a perfect finish to a satisfying Mexican meal.

SERVES 6 TO 8

2 pounds yellow guavas

3/4 cup brown sugar, loosely packed

1 Bosc pear, unpeeled, cored and cut into 3/4-inch cubes

A 3-inch piece canela, broken in half

Zest of 1/2 lime (see Cooking Notes below)

Juice of 1 lime

1/2 cup sour cream

Clean the guavas, removing the dead flower and loose rind from the end. Do not peel. Trim the tops and cut the guavas in half crosswise. Using a grapefruit spoon or a spoon with a thin edge, remove the seeds from the guava halves. This can be done easily by turning the spoon around the visible perimeter of the seed area and then scraping out any remaining seeds with the tip of the spoon. After cleaning, you will have hollow hemispheres lined with 1/8-1/4 inch of seedless guava flesh. Set aside.

Choose a skillet large enough to later hold all of the guavas in a single layer. Heat the skillet over high heat and add 2 1/2 cups of cold water, the brown sugar and canela. Stir to dissolve the sugar, bring the mixture to a fast boil and cook until slightly thickened, about 5 minutes.

Add the guavas to the skillet with the hollow sides facing down. Sprinkle the pear chunks into the space between the guavas. Reduce the heat to medium-high, cover and cook for 10 minutes. Uncover and sprinkle the lime zest over the guava tops. Using a spoon, carefully turn over each guava and pear piece. Squeeze the lime juice over the top. Add a couple of tablespoons of water if the syrup starts to dry out. Cover the skillet and cook until the guavas are soft and pliable but not falling apart, 5-10 minutes depending on their size. Carefully place the guavas with the cut side up into individual compote dishes. Spoon the pear chunks attractively around the guavas. The syrup in the skillet should be thick like maple syrup, and show a froth of large bubbles on its surface as it is boiling. If the syrup is too thin, continue to reduce over high heat until it shows the bubbly froth. If it is too thick, add 2-3 tablespoons of water, scrape the skillet with a wooden spatula to loosen the paste and stir to mix. Pour the syrup into the guava halves and spoon small dollops of sour cream into the centers of each guava. Serve hot.

Cooking Notes

Zesting Citrus Fruits: Use a vegetable peeler or zester to remove only the colored portion of the peel, not the bitter white pith underneath. The zest may then be minced, or simply cut into thin julienne strips.

Creamy Peppermint Gelatin With Mexican Chocolate Sauce

Gelatin of all sorts are popular and refreshing desserts in Mexico. This peppermint-pink rendition has a little spice added by freshly ground cloves. Served with a sauce of Mexican chocolate, it makes a delightful finish to a substantial meal. The question will not be whether to have a second helping, but how much to have!

SERVES 6

For the Peppermint Gelatin
Safflower oil for coating ramekins
2 1/2 cups whole milk
2 envelopes unflavored gelatin
6 1/2 ounces peppermint candies
12 whole cloves
1 tablespoon molasses (optional)
2/3 cup whipping cream

Preparing the Gelatin: Coat 6 single-serving ramekins with safflower oil and set them aside. Place 1/2 cup cold milk in a small bowl. Sprinkle the surface with the gelatin and let it stand until softened, about 5 minutes. Coarsely crush the peppermint candies in a food processor, or wrap in a towel and break the candies with a meat tenderizer. In a large bowl, prepare an ice water bath.

Prepare the cloves in a bouquet garni (see Cooking Notes, page 25), or prepare a strainer to remove them later. In a medium saucepan over medium heat, combine the remaining milk, the crushed peppermint candies, the bouquet garni and the optional molasses. Stir to dissolve the candy. Do not allow the milk to come to a boil. Add the gelatin mixture to the pan, stir to combine and remove from the heat. Place the saucepan in the ice water bath until the gelatin is the consistency of raw egg whites, about 15 minutes. Meanwhile, use an electric mixer to beat the whipping cream in a cold metal bowl until stiff peaks form. Remove the bouquet garni or strain the loose cloves from the gelatin mixture, and fold the whipped cream into the gelatin until evenly incorporated. Pour the peppermint mixture into the prepared ramekins, cover and refrigerate until firm, about 2 hours. If you are in a hurry, place the ramekins in the freezer for 30 minutes, then transfer them to the refrigerator for another 30 minutes before serving.

For the Mexican Chocolate Sauce
3 ounces Mexican-style chocolate, finely chopped or in powdered form
1/4 cup unsweetened cocoa powder

Preparing the Chocolate Sauce: In a small saucepan over low heat, combine the chocolate, cocoa powder and 1/2 cup of water, stirring until smooth, about 5 minutes. Make sure the coarse sugar from the Mexican chocolate has dissolved before removing the chocolate sauce from the heat.

For Assembly
Garnish: 6 sprigs fresh mint

Assembling the Dish: To serve, run a knife along the inside edge of a ramekin and jiggle it a little to loosen the gelatin. Cover the ramekin with a dessert plate, invert and remove the ramekin. Repeat with the remaining ramekins. Pour a pool of the warm chocolate sauce around the outer perimeter of each dessert gelatin, garnish with a mint sprig and serve.

Jamaica "Flower" & Raspberry Sorbet

NIEVE DE JAMAICA Y FRAMBUESA

The inspiration for this intensely colored sorbet is a "paleta," similar to a pop-sicle but much better. Paletas are available in special stores all over Mexico, but are made especially well in Puebla. Tamarind, jamaica, melon and lime are just a few of the flavors available. This sorbet pairs jamaica "flowers," also known as hibiscus, with raspberries, a refreshing combination with which to end any meal.

SERVES 4 ♦ YIELDS APPROXIMATELY 2 1/2 CUPS

1/2 cup jamaica "flowers" (about 1/2 ounce)

3/4 cup sugar

1 1/2 cups raspberry purée, unsweetened (about 12 ounces fresh or thawed)

2 tablespoons fresh lime juice

1 tablespoon tequila (optional)

Garnish:

1 mango and 1 kiwi, each peeled and cut into 1/2-inch cubes

4 fresh mint sprigs

In a medium saucepan over high heat, combine the jamaica with 1 3/4 cups of cold water. Bring to a boil and cook for 2 minutes. Add the sugar and stir until dissolved, 1-2 minutes. Remove from the heat and steep for 2 hours.

Strain the liquid into a bowl and discard the flowers. Stir in the raspberry purée, lime juice and optional tequila. Cover with plastic and refrigerate for 1 hour. Stir again, pour the mixture into an ice cream maker and follow the man-ufacturer's instructions. An alternative freezing method is to pour the liquid into a shallow, non-metallic bowl, cover and place in the freezer for 4 hours. Whisk the mixture after the second hour, and again after the third hour, in order to break apart ice crystals so that the sorbet can be scooped. Serve in small dish-es, topped with the fruit and mint sprigs.

Mexican Hot Chocolate

CHOCOLATE

"WE HUMBLY KNEEL TO GRIND THEE
WE FOLD OUR HANDS IN PRAYER TO WHIP THEE
AND RAISE OUR EYES TO THE HEAVENS TO DRINK THEE"
- Zapotec proverb for traditional chocolate making & drinking

Chocolate was first sampled by the Spanish in Montezuma's court. A highly regarded drink for both ceremony and pleasure, it was consumed from golden cups. Surprisingly, it took two centuries for the drink to catch on in Europe, but when it did, everyone went mad for the stuff. In Mexico, chocolate has remained a simple drink made with milk or water, or even beaten with corn masa to make "champurrado." Chocolate is also used as an ingredient in savory foods, such as Roasted Turkey with Mole Poblano (page 77).

Traditionally, this chocolate drink is beaten to a froth with a "molinillo," a stick with a carved rattle on the end, designed to trap air and beat it into the drink (that's the folding hands in prayer part). But, don't worry, a blender works too. Mexican traditionalists also say, "Chocolate should only be beaten by the hands of a woman." Only feminine grace can make the drink taste just right!

SERVES 3 TO 4 ♦ YIELDS 3 CUPS

2 1/2 cups lowfat milk

2 3-inch pieces canela

3 ounces Mexican-style chocolate, finely chopped or in powdered form

Heat a small, preferably non-stick saucepan over medium heat. When hot, add the milk and canela. Stir, raise the heat to medium-high, bring the milk to a boil and continue boiling for 2 minutes. Add the chocolate and stir frequently until it is completely melted. Remove the canela and discard. Transfer the chocolate to a blender and beat to a froth, about 30 seconds. Serve hot.

Refreshing Drink of Jamaica "Flowers"

Jamaica "flowers," also called hibiscus, are not actually flowers. The "flower" is really a calyx—the part of the plant enclosing a bloom. Jamaica is high in vitamin C and makes an exceedingly refreshing drink. It is an immeasurably appreciated alternative to iced tea during lunch or dinner, and is also wonderful after a dehydrating experience, such as exercise or sitting in the hot sun.

S E R V E S   4   T O   6   ♦   Y I E L D S   4   1 / 2   C U P S

1/2 cup jamaica "flowers" (about 1/2 ounce)

6 tablespoons sugar

1/2 cup fresh lime juice (about 2-4 limes)

Garnish: Lime slices

In a medium saucepan, bring 6 cups of cold water to a boil over high heat. Add the jamaica flowers, stir and return to a boil. Reduce the heat to low, cover and simmer for 15 minutes. Add the sugar and stir until dissolved. Remove from the heat and allow to steep. When cool, strain out the flowers and discard them if you wish. Stir in the lime juice and chill. Serve over ice, garnished with the slices of lime.